3ds Max ANIMATION WITH Biped

W0010412

Michele Bousquet
Michael McCarthy

New Riders

3ds Max Animation with Biped

Michele Bousquet and Michael McCarthy

New Riders
1249 Eighth Street
Berkeley, CA 94710
510/524-2178
800/283-9444
510/524-2221 (fax)

Find us on the World Wide Web at: www.newriders.com
To report errors, please send a note to errata@peachpit.com

New Riders is an imprint of Peachpit, a division of Pearson Education

Editor: Kate McKinley
Project Editor: Paula Baker
Production Editor: Simmy Cover
Contributor: Mark Gerhard
Technical Editor: Jon McFarland
Compositors: Robin Kibby and Kate Kaminski, Happenstance Type-O-Rama
Indexer: Karin Arrigoni
Cover Design: Mimi Heft
Cover Production: Andreas F. Schueller
Interior design: Maureen Forys, Happenstance Type-O-Rama

Thanks to Dosch Designs for providing their great cartoon models.
DOSCH DESIGN www.doschdesign.com

ISBN 0-321-37572-6

9 8 7 6 5 4 3 2 1

Printed and bound in the United States of America

CONTENTS

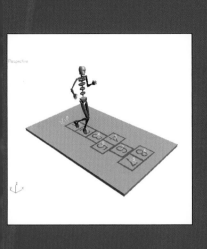

Introduction

Welcome to the world of 3ds Max and Biped!

Biped is a subject with many facets. If you are new to this software, understanding a little of its history and usage will help you use the software more effectively. Biped, along with Physique, was a component of Character Studio, which has now been incorporated into 3ds Max.

A Brief History of Character Animation

Character animation with 3D software is a relatively new art form. In 3D, animating a character is quite different from animating a bouncing ball or a car rolling down the street. A living creature has limbs that move in various ways. When it walks or runs, at least one body part (such as the left or right foot) reacts with the ground at any given time.

Throughout the 1990s, three different approaches were developed to make 3D character animation possible: jointed characters, model controls, and skeletons.

Jointed Characters

The first approach was to create jointed characters, similar to a marionette. The parts were linked together in a hierarchy; moving the torso would move the entire character in space. Then the arms and legs could be rotated separately.

This solution is still in use for many types of animation, but it has limitations. The joints are nearly always visible, or become visible as soon as the character starts to move. Animators can get around this problem by fitting the character with certain types of clothing or armor, or by animating the character very carefully (and tediously). Because of the joints' visibility, this type of animation is currently used only with action figures wearing armor, and with characters that are supposed to look like marionettes.

Another limitation of jointed animation is the hierarchy itself. As soon as the torso moves, the feet move. This makes it hard to pin the feet to the ground when the character is walking or moving around. Some tools were developed in the 1990s for pinning the feet down, but these were often awkward and hard to use.

Model Controls

To get around the problems of joints, another approach was developed for one-piece character models. An animator could place controls at key points on a character's body and use the controls to push and pull parts of the mesh.

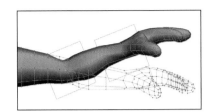

Although this technique makes it possible to animate a character smoothly, it is also tedious and difficult. A great number of controls is necessary to make the character deform correctly; and when animated the character can seem to be made of rubber or clay. Also, with model controls it takes a very long time to do just a few seconds of animation.

Animators have always been inventive in their use of jointed characters and model controls. With extensive controls and scripting, it was (and still is) possible for an animator to create a custom tool set that speeds up the animation process and gets better results. However, not everyone has the time or the means to learn scripting and write their own tools.

Skeletons and Skinning

A third approach was developed that mirrors real life more closely. A skeletal structure is placed inside the character model. When the skeleton is animated, it acts like bones inside a body and causes the character model to deform accordingly.

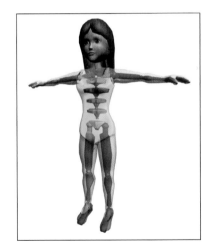

This technique requires tools to make the skeleton affect the character model appropriately. For example, the skeleton's upper arm bone must affect just the character's upper arm and no other body part.

As skeleton tools developed, new terminology was introduced. The objects that make up the skeleton are often called *bones*. The association of a skeleton with a character model is called *skinning*. If an animator is going to "skin a character," the animator is going to create a skeleton and associate the skeleton with the character model.

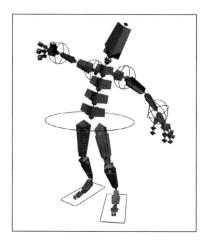

In the 1990s, new objects called *Bones* were introduced in 3ds Max. These objects were automatically linked together as they were created, making it easier to create a skeleton. In addition, plug-ins became available for skinning characters in 3ds Max.

Even with improved tools, the animator still had to construct the skeleton manually with Bones or other 3ds Max objects, and also had to create his or her own controls for animating the skeleton. Designing such controls is time consuming and can be daunting for the new animator.

To solve all these problems, Character Studio was introduced.

Character Studio

►TIP◄

To learn how to animate with Bones rather than a biped, see the "Resources" appendix.

In 1995, the first version of Character Studio was released as a plug-in for 3ds Max. The software was revolutionary in that it provided all the elements an animator needed to do character animation quickly and easily:

- A full humanoid skeleton that can easily be posed to fit most types of characters

- Tools for skinning a character

- Animation tools for the skeleton

- Easy methods for making the feet stick to the ground when necessary

- Methods for reusing animation that has already been created

Of these, the last two elements are perhaps the most important. With Character Studio, an animator can take a character model and make it walk around in a matter of minutes rather than hours or days. An animator no longer has to be an expert at scripting to get good results with character animation. Once the motions are created, they can be reused for other animation sequences.

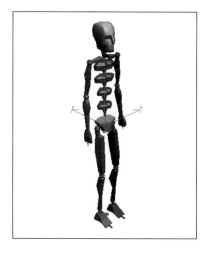

The Character Studio skeleton is called a *biped*, which means "two-footed."

Biped Today

Character Studio has been included with 3ds Max versions 7 and later instead of being available only as a plug-in. Its name no longer appears in the 3ds Max software itself, although you might find "Character Studio" in the 3ds Max documentation.

The key feature of Character Studio is its *Biped* module. This part of the software deals exclusively with the creation and animation of the biped skeleton. Most of this book is devoted to Biped tools and techniques. Because it gives results so quickly, the Biped module and its animation techniques are very popular with game developers and film/TV animators.

The *Physique* modifier is also part of Character Studio. This modifier skins a character with any skeleton, regardless of whether it is a biped or a custom skeleton made of 3ds Max objects.

Nowadays, the *Skin* modifier is included with 3ds Max. Like Physique, the Skin modifier skins a character. In 3ds Max 5 and later, Skin has been improved to the degree that it is superior to Physique. In general, animators use Physique rather than Skin only when they have a need for features specific to Physique, such as automatic muscle bulges.

When we refer to Character Studio in this book, we are referring to the Biped module and Physique modifier that are included with 3ds Max.

Biped Basics

There are a few concepts you should understand before you get started with *3ds Max Animation with Biped*.

Terminology

When you see the term *Biped* with a capital *B*, this refers to the Biped module and its tools. The term *biped* with a lowercase *b* refers to the biped skeleton itself.

In any software package, the term *rig* refers to a set of controls for animating a character. A rig consists of a skeleton and the controls for animating the skeleton. A biped skeleton includes a complete rig.

Choosing a Mesh

Before working with the Biped software, you need a mesh to work with. Character Studio does not create meshes, nor does it have any tools for doing so. There are a number of ways to find a character mesh suitable for animation with Biped, and you'll find a few ideas in the "Resources" appendix.

Another option is creating your own character from scratch, but keep in mind that learning how to do this takes time. Even when you become adept at creating characters, it can take days or weeks to create an appealing, believable character that will animate well. Common methods for character creation are box modeling and surface modeling with the Surface modifier. (See the "Resources" appendix for some recommended books on modeling.)

When you first start working with character design and animation, it's a good idea to use meshes from another source. After you learn more about how characters are animated, it will be easier for you to make usable character meshes.

Setting Up the Mesh

For a character mesh to work well with Biped, a few setup actions are needed. The mesh must be properly positioned and scaled before you can associate it with your biped.

To begin working with a character, you load it into 3ds Max. You can also have other objects in your scene, such as an environment to work in.

The character mesh should be positioned with its head facing forward, arms outstretched, and palms facing down. The legs should have a little distance between them. If your mesh isn't in this position, you will have to move and rotate vertices until it is. All of the meshes that come with 3ds Max are in this pose.

▶QUICKLIST◀

CHARACTER MESH SETUP

❑ Pose the character with its head facing forward and its arms outstretched, palms facing down.

❑ If necessary, scale the character to fit the scene *before* starting to work on it.

❑ Rotate the mesh so it's facing the Front viewport.

❑ Move the mesh so it's standing on the construction plane.

❑ Create a named selection set for the mesh.

The mesh doesn't have to be all in one piece. Biped will work equally well with one- and multiple-piece characters. You'll find out how this works later in the book.

Before using the character, you might need to scale it to fit the environment. Attempting to scale a character after manipulating it with Biped can have unpredictable results. You won't have to perform this scaling step in any of the exercises in this book, but you should be aware of its necessity in some situations.

It will be easier to work with the biped if you first rotate the mesh so it's facing the Front viewport. It's also a good idea to move the mesh so that it's standing on the construction plane, if this suits your environment. Once the mesh is placed, freeze it so that you won't accidentally select it when working with the biped.

Your work will be made much easier if you create a *named selection set* for the mesh. This will enable you to easily and quickly select the mesh later on.

Production Workflow

The list of steps included here will give you an idea of how Character Studio works. You can also use it as a reference as you go through this book, and afterward when working on your own animation.

1. **CREATE OR OBTAIN A MESH.** Create a character mesh, or retrieve one from the Internet or some other source.

2. **CREATE A BIPED.** This is a quick step—just a click and a drag to make the biped skeleton.

3. **CHANGE BIPED PARAMETERS.** Set up the biped with the appropriate number of fingers and toes, spine links, and so on.

4. **FIT BIPED TO MESH.** Move, rotate, and scale the biped until it fits inside the mesh like a real skeleton.

5. **ASSOCIATE BIPED AND MESH.** Use the Skin modifier or Physique modifier to associate the biped with the mesh.

6. **MAKE PRELIMINARY SKINNING ADJUSTMENTS.** The default settings for both Skin and Physique usually require adjustments to make the biped affect the mesh correctly. You can make some preliminary adjustments at this point, even before you animate the biped.

7. **CREATE A TEST ANIMATION FOR THE BIPED.** You can create a quick footstep animation, a more customized animation using the freeform method, or some combination of the two.

8. **WATCH THE ANIMATION TO SEE THE DEFORMATION.** Some parts of the mesh won't behave as expected when the biped moves, indicating that more adjustments are needed in the Skin or Physique modifier.

9. **CREATE THE FINAL ANIMATION.** Create the actual animation that you want the biped to perform. This could include crowd scenes, or mixing motions to create a complex animation.

10. **RENDER THE ANIMATION.** Hide the biped and render the mesh in its environment.

In this book you'll learn how to do all these steps, plus a few other tricks that Biped has to offer.

Using This Book

Each section of *3ds Max Animation with Biped* covers a different technique for working with the Biped software: Skinning, Footsteps, Freeform Animation, and Combining Motions. The chapters cover various tasks you can accomplish with those techniques, and exercises will walk you through the process of using the associated tools.

The exercises are meant to be performed using 3ds Max version 8, but some may also work in earlier versions. However, the Max files on the accompanying CD were all saved in version 8 and will not open in earlier versions.

WORD TO THE WISE: If you're using 3ds Max 8, be sure to get the Service Pack 1 update, which fixes a number of bugs.

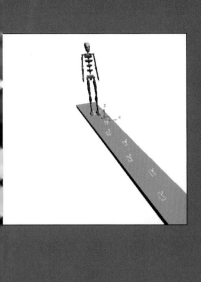

SECTION I

Getting Started

Character Studio has a wide variety of features for making characters walk, run, jump, climb, fight, and do most anything. Before you jump in and play with its features, use this section to learn the overall workflow and get some results right away.

In this section, you'll make a character walk around with a minimum of clicks, and find out how Character Studio sets its keys for such an animation. You'll also learn how to manipulate the Character Studio skeleton (called the *biped*), and how to associate it with a character mesh.

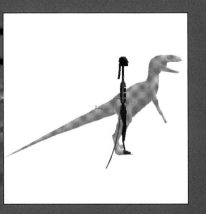

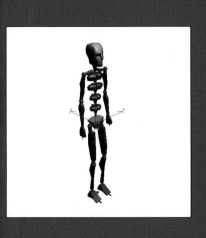

CHAPTER 1

Character Studio Basics

In this chapter, you'll get a character to walk around with just a few steps. Then you'll learn how Character Studio creates this animation. You'll also learn the basic workflow for working with Character Studio's many features.

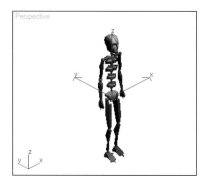

Quick Start

Want to get started right away? You can follow this quick set of steps to get some action with Character Studio in just a few minutes.

1. Create a biped. On the [icon] Create panel go to [icon] Systems > Biped, then drag out a biped in the Perspective viewport.

2. Go to the [icon] Motion panel. As long as any part of the biped is still selected, you will see the Biped rollout.

3. On the Biped rollout click [icon] Footstep Mode.

   The Footstep Creation rollout appears.

4. Click [icon] Create Multiple Footsteps. In the Create Multiple Footsteps: Walk dialog click OK.

   This creates footstep icons in the scene. If you click Play Animation, nothing happens. That's because you have to create keys for the footsteps.

5. To see the footsteps better, turn off the axis tripod display. To do this, choose Views menu > Show Transform Gizmo.

6. Click [icon] Create Keys for Inactive Footsteps.

7. Click [icon] Play Animation to watch the biped walk.

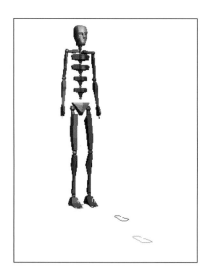

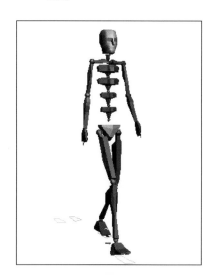

Biped Basics

A *biped* is a set of linked objects that you can use as a skeleton for a character. The default skeleton contains humanoid body parts such as a head, spine, arms, and legs.

Optionally, you may add a tail and other nonhuman body parts.

Although a biped consists of several objects, it is created as a single unit. You can set certain parameters such as the number of fingers and toes, but the biped is required to have certain parts such as a head, spine, and legs. You can hide these parts if you don't want them in your scene.

Sometimes you'll want to add 3ds Max Bones to a biped skeleton to animate wings, jaws, or ears or to create facial expression animations.

►TIP◄

In plain English, the term *biped* refers to something with two feet.

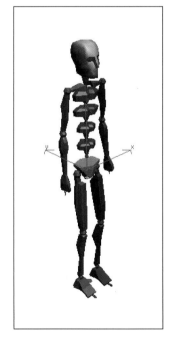

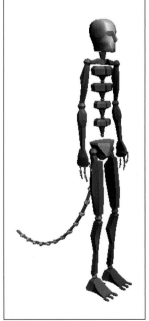

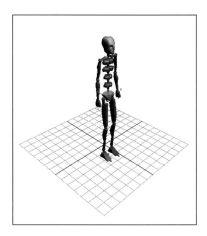

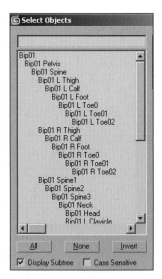

EXERCISE 1.1

Changing the Biped Structure

1. Reset 3ds Max.

2. To create a biped, go to the [icon] Create panel > [icon] Systems > Biped. Click and drag in any viewport to create the biped on the construction grid.

No matter which viewport you use to create the biped, it is always created standing upright along the Z axis, and standing on the XY construction grid. The biped must stand in this direction so it is ready to work with Character Studio's gravity computations, which are computed along the Z axis by default.

3. Go to the [icon] Motion panel.

4. You should see the Biped controls on the Motion panel. If the Motion panel shows the regular 3ds Max object controls rather than the Biped controls, select any biped part to make them appear.

The Biped controls appear on the Motion panel only when at least one biped part is selected.

5. In the Biped rollout, click [icon] Figure mode. Then you can change the biped's attributes in the Structure rollout.

6. Click [icon] Select by Name on the main toolbar (or press the H key) to see the names of the objects that make up the biped. Then in the Select Objects dialog, turn on the Display Subtree option. Note how the objects are indented on the list. Objects are indented under the objects they are linked to. All object names should begin with the prefix Bip01.

Linking and Hierarchies

Linking creates a relationship between two objects, allowing you to control one object by moving or rotating the other. The biped is automatically linked together when you create it.

A linear series of linked objects is called a *chain*. Two or more chains linked together are called a *hierarchy*. The higher object in a chain or hierarchy is called the *parent* object, and any object linked under it is a *child* object. A parent can also be the child of another object (linked under it), and a child object can be the parent of another object.

When you view the biped hierarchy, you can see that there is one object that is only a parent, and not a child to any other object. This object is called the *root* of the hierarchy. Every hierarchy has only one root.

With the biped, the root is the object at the top of the list, Bip01. This is the center of mass (COM) of the object, shown as a small diamond shape inside the biped's pelvis. It can be used to move or rotate the entire biped.

You'll learn more about biped parts in Chapter 2. For now, let's work with the default biped a little to see how it can be animated.

Animating a Biped

Animating a character's upper body is a pretty simple process. You simply turn on Auto Key and move and rotate the bones (or biped parts) as you would any other 3ds Max object.

The legs are another matter. As the character walks, runs, jumps, climbs, or dances, the feet stick and unstick themselves from the floor (or, in the case of climbing, the ladder or tree). At certain parts of the animation, one or both feet are stuck down while the body continues to move. In other words, the feet are continually sticking and unsticking themselves from something while the body moves around them.

The problem of how to make the feet stick at the right times is not a new one in 3D animation. Perhaps you have seen animation where the character's feet seem to slide as the character crosses the floor, or maybe you have run into this problem in your own animation.

Kinematics

In the world of 3D animation, the term *kinematics* describes the movement of a linked structure. There are two types of kinematics that can be used with linked objects: forward kinematics (FK) and inverse kinematics (IK).

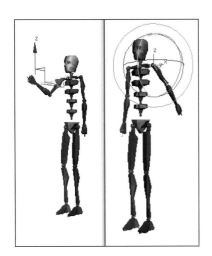

With *forward kinematics*, when a parent in the chain moves or rotates, the children under it also move or rotate. This was the only method of kinematics available in the early days of computer animation, and it still has many uses.

With *inverse kinematics*, you can move a child object and have the parent objects rotate accordingly. For example, you could move a character's foot to cause the thigh and calf to move and rotate appropriately.

One of the primary tasks of Character Studio is to simplify the process of sticking and unsticking the feet at the right times. This is accomplished by switching between forward kinematics and inverse kinematics in a linked chain.

While you're animating, Biped switches between FK and IK depending on what you're doing. An easy way to see this feature in action is to rotate one of the biped's feet. When you *rotate* the foot, only the foot is affected, which is FK. When you *move* the foot, the entire leg rotates to accommodate the new foot position, which is IK.

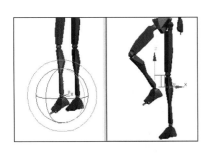

When animated with IK, the hand or foot is called an *end effector*. An end effector is the child object on the chain that, when moved, affects parent objects in the chain. The biped swaps between FK and IK automatically depending on whether you're *moving* or *rotating* the end effector.

In order for the automatic swap between FK and IK to work during the animation process, certain limitations are imposed.

- IK is only in effect when part of a leg or arm is moved. At all other times, FK is in effect. For example, if a hand or arm is rotated rather than moved, FK is used.

- When IK is in effect, the animation is only passed so far up the chain. For example, if you move the biped's foot, the leg moves and rotates accordingly, but the COM and spine do not.

- Some body parts can only be rotated. These include the spine, head, neck, and any tail or ponytail links. These parts all use FK only.

If the concept of FK and IK is new to you, you can remember the limitations with these simple rules.

- Arms and legs, and anything that extends from them (hands, fingers, feet, and toes) can use FK or IK. All other body parts use FK only.

- Rotate = FK, Move = IK.

You can use IK to make a character's feet stick and unstick from the ground using the controls on the Key Info rollout. With Character Studio, you can instruct the biped to hold one or both of its feet still for any number of frames while the rest of the body responds to FK around it. Let's try this now.

EXERCISE 1.2

Kinematics and the Biped

In this exercise, you'll use IK and FK with the Biped, and see how it responds.

Set a Key at Frame 0

1. Reset 3ds Max.

2. Create a biped of any size in a viewport.

3. Go to the ⊛ Motion panel.

   Here you'll find a number of colorful buttons that aren't there for ordinary 3ds Max objects. The biped has its own Motion panel, complete with FK and IK controls.

4. On the Track Selection rollout, click ↔ Body Horizontal.

►TIP◄

If you don't see the Biped buttons, select any part of the biped to make the buttons appear.

This selects the COM (center of mass), or Bip01. Turn Show Transform Gizmo back on, so you can see the selection.

5.   Expand the Key Info rollout.

6.   While on frame 0, click the [◉] Set Key button on the Key Info rollout.

The Set Key button sets a key regardless of whether Auto Key is on or off. In this case, you have just set a key for the COM at frame 0.

Animate the COM with FK

►NOTE◄

Don't confuse the Set Key button on the Key Info rollout with the Set Key button near the track bar. Character Studio does not work well with the standard 3ds Max Set Key button. Avoid using it with biped animation.

►TIP◄

Biped doesn't follow the standard 3ds Max behavior of automatically setting a key at frame 0 when you set a key at another frame. Get in the habit of manually setting keys at frame 0 when you start your animation—you'll be happy you did.

1.   Turn on Auto Key by clicking the [Auto Key] Auto Key button near the bottom of the screen.

2.   Move the time slider to frame 10.

3.   In the Left viewport, move the COM to the right.

4.   Scrub (pull) the time slider.

The entire biped moves between frames 0 and 10. The COM works with FK, which means it moves all its child objects with it. Since the COM is the root of the hierarchy, the entire biped moves when you move the COM.

Set a Key for the Leg

Now we'll set some keys for one of the feet and see what happens.

1.   Select any part of the right leg (the green leg).

2.   On frame 0, click the [◉] Set Key button on the Key Info rollout.

This sets a key for the leg on frame 0. There is one key for the entire leg. If you select any other part of the right leg, you will see that there is a key for that object on the track bar.

3.   Go to frame 10.

4.   Click the [◉] Set Key button again.

5.   Pull the time slider to see the animation.

The leg is still following the COM, indicating that it is still under the control of FK. When you set a key for the leg with the Set Key button, an FK key is set by default. Let's put in an IK key now.

Set an IK Key for the Foot

1. Go to frame 10.

2. Select any part of the right leg or foot.

3. In the Key Info rollout, click the ⬚ Set Planted Key button.

   This sets an IK key on the foot that makes it "stick" right where it is.

4. Expand the IK section of the Key Info rollout by clicking the + next to the section name.

   You will now see additional controls for making the extremities stick to objects or to the world. The Set Planted Key button has automatically set IK Blend to 1.0, and selected the Object space option. It also turned on Join to Prev IK Key. You will learn more about what these options mean in the next section.

5. Go to frame 20.

6. In the Track Selection rollout, click ↔ Body Horizontal to select the COM.

7. In the Left viewport, move the COM slightly downward and to the right.

   As you can see, the right foot stays stuck down, while the rest of the body moves with the COM. The left leg moves with the COM because it is still under the control of FK.

8. Turn AutoKey off.

> ►NOTE◄
>
> You can use the ⬚ Set Free Key button to change the settings to FK settings rather than IK. This button automatically sets IK Blend to 0.0 and selects the Body option. Then the foot uses FK and follows the COM, and the foot becomes "unstuck" from the world.

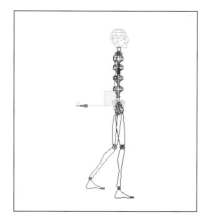

Creating a Walk Cycle

You could set a series of FK and IK keys to make the biped walk, but this would become repetitive and tedious. Character Studio is designed to automate repetitive tasks, including this one.

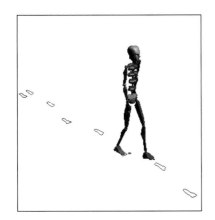

Biped uses *footsteps* to help you make the biped walk around. This automatically sets IK and FK keys for the legs, as well as FK keys for the rest of the body. It adds arm-swinging animation, also—and tail-swinging if a tail is present. Footstep icons look like footprints, with green and blue footsteps denoting right and left footsteps respectively.

EXERCISE 1.3

IK and FK Keys for Biped

In this exercise, you'll use footsteps to make the biped walk around. Then you'll look at the IK and FK keys created.

Make the Biped Walk with Footsteps

1. Reset 3ds Max.

2. In any viewport, create a biped.

3. Go to the [icon] Motion panel.

4. In the Biped rollout, click [icon] Footstep Mode to turn it on.

   A new set of rollouts are now available.

5. In the Footstep Creation rollout, click [icon] Create Multiple Footsteps.

   This displays the Create Multiple Footsteps: Walk dialog.

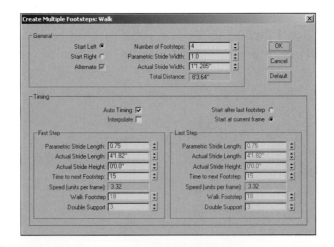

6. In the Create Multiple Footsteps: Walk dialog, change Number of Footsteps to 8, and click OK.

   A series of footstep icons appear in the viewports.

7. Click in a blank area of a viewport to unselect the footsteps.

   The footsteps are placed in front of the biped, with green footsteps for the right foot and blue footsteps for the left. Each footstep has a number from 0 to 7 to indicate the sequence of steps. The footsteps don't affect the biped yet because keys haven't been created for them.

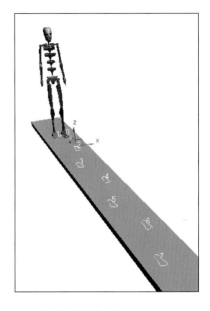

8. In the Footstep Operations rollout, click [icon] Create Keys for Inactive Footsteps.

   This creates keys for the biped's legs, arms, and other components, as well as for the COM.

9. Click [icon] Play Animation to play the animation.

   The biped steps through the footsteps.

   That was quick, wasn't it? But if you look closely, the walk is a bit stiff. The arms don't swing uniformly, and the hip and shoulder motions are robotic.

   Although Character Studio is quick with automating repetitive tasks, it is not designed to replace an animator's talent. This quick walk cycle is a starting point, not the end of the job.

   Later, we will discuss how to make the walk cycle look more professional, and suitable for a demo reel. But for now, you can see that the task of making the feet stick and unstick at the appropriate times has been taken care of for you.

► TIP ◄

Beginner animators are often excited about the idea of using default footstep animation on their demo reels. This is not a good idea. Any studio recruiter can spot an unembellished Character Studio footstep cycle a mile away, and they will toss your demo reel in the trash.

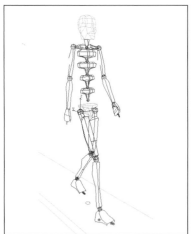

Look at the IK Keys

What have the footsteps really accomplished in terms of the IK and FK keys? You can find out by converting the footsteps to a freeform animation. In Biped, *freeform* is a catch-all term for animation that doesn't use footsteps.

1. On the Biped Rollout click ▐▌ Footstep Mode to turn it off.

2. In the Biped rollout, click ▐▌ Convert. On the Convert to freeform dialog, click OK without changing the settings.

   The footsteps disappear from the viewports.

3. Play the animation.

   The biped walks exactly the same way as it did before. However, the footsteps have been removed. The animation has been converted to use just FK and IK settings.

4. Select any part of the right leg and go to the Key Info rollout. If necessary, expand the IK bar on the Key Info rollout so you can see the IK Blend parameter.

5. Pull the time slider while watching the IK Blend parameter and Body/Object settings.

   When the right foot sticks down, IK Blend is 1.0 and the Object option is selected. When the right foot moves through the air, IK Blend is 0.0 and the Body option is selected.

   These parameter settings show what footsteps actually do. They automatically set up FK and IK on the legs to make the biped walk. Creating keys for footsteps also sets keys for the arms and COM to make them move when the biped walks.

   The planted keys also display a red dot in the viewports indicating the pivot point as the biped moves. If you select both feet and play the animation, you will see the red dot jumping from foot to foot, indicating where the planted pivot is set on any given frame.

Building a Better Walk Cycle

You can take the default walk cycle that Character Studio produces, and use that as the foundation for your animation work. There are many ways to make changes to the default walk cycle. We'll look at a simple approach here. We'll simply find the points when the feet are locked to the ground, and lower the COM at those frames using the Set Multiple Keys feature. Then we'll add extra movement in the spine, arms, and head.

Adjusting the Stride

1. Reset 3ds Max.

2. Create a biped with a height of 60 units. When you drag out the biped watch the Height field change as you move your cursor. Stop close to 60, then use the spinner or highlight the field and type in 60.

3. In the Motion Panel, click ![footstep icon] Footstep Mode.

4. In the Footstep Creation rollout, click ![multiple footsteps icon] Create Multiple Footsteps.

5. Set the Number of Footsteps to 10.

6. Set the Actual Stride Width to 4.0, and Actual Stride Length to 30.

   The Actual Stride parameters let you set the stride values in actual 3ds Max units. If you are working in a particular scale this can be handy to enter real-world measurements here.

7. Set Time to next Footstep to 13. Click OK.

   This will create a walk cycle that's a little faster and more energetic than the one you made previously.

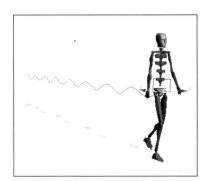

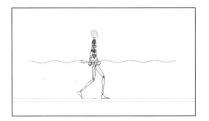

8. Click [icon] Create Keys for Inactive Footsteps to animate the biped walking. This takes the footstep information and generates the biped animation based on the footstep placement and orientation.

9. Turn off Footstep mode then [icon] play the animation.

   Note that the time segment has been extended to 132 to accomodate the extra animation.

Using Trajectories and Key Mode

Sometimes it's helpful to see the path that a biped body part follows through space. Biped has a Trajectories button that works well for this purpose.

1. Select the COM. In the Biped rollout, expand the Modes and Display section, then in the Display group turn on [icon] Trajectories.

2. To ensure that you only adjust existing keys, turn on the [icon] Key Mode Toggle.

3. Press the > key on the keyboard repeatedly to move through the animation.

   Look at the biped in the Left viewport, and move to each key frame for the COM. The COM is at its lowest point at frames 29, 41, 54, 67, 80, 93, 106, and 119.

4. Turn on Auto Key, then go to frame 29.

5. In the Track Selection rollout, select the [icon] Body Vertical button. In the Left viewport, move the COM downward by approximately 3 units. The feet are locked to the ground, so the leg links rotate as the COM is lowered.

6. On the track bar, select keys 41, 54, 67, 80, 93, 106, and 119. You can do this by holding the Ctrl key while clicking each one.

   The selected keys turn white to indicate they are selected.

7. With these multiple keys selected, expand the Keyframing Tools rollout and click ⊞ Set Multiple Keys.

8. In the Biped Multiple Keys dialog, click Apply Increment once.

   The biped COM is lowered on all the selected keys at once.

9. Play the animation. The biped has more bounce in his step.

10. In the Track Selection rollout, select the ↻ Body Rotation button.

11. Use the > key on the keyboard to advance keyframe by keyframe. At each keyframe where the COM is lowered, rotate the COM about its X axis so the biped leans slightly toward the extended foot. Alternate rotating left and right, depending on which foot is extended.

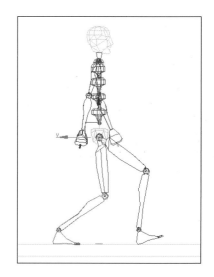

12. Play the animation. The biped now has a goofy walk.

13. Close the Biped Multiple Keys dialog.

Adding arm and head movement

1. Select the Bip01 Spine object. This is the lowest spine link on the biped.

2. On the same keyframes you adjusted for the COM before, rotate the Bipo1 Spine object about its X and Y axis so the arms swing in synchronization with the leg movements.

3. Repeat the process for the upper arms so they swing even more. With Auto Key still on, reposition the arms so they swing farther back on the backswing, and closer to the chest on the upswing.

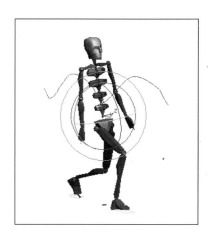

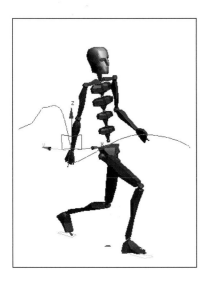

4. The last thing to do is to add some movement to the head. At the same key frames, rotate the Bip01 head object about 10 degrees to counterbalance the hip and shoulder movement. Alternate directions of the rotation as you like.

5. Save (Ctrl+S) your file as `mygoofywalk.max`.

6. You don't have to keep this a footstep animation. In the Biped rollout click ⏣ Convert and then OK in the Convert to Freeform dialog. The footsteps are now gone.

   If you like you can load `goofywalk.max` from the CD to compare it with your own file.

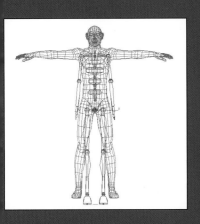

CHAPTER 2

Posing the Biped

Before you can associate the biped with your character model, you must pose the biped to fit the mesh. This includes adding and removing parts as needed and changing the sizes of biped parts to fit the mesh. A superhero biped looks very different from a biped for an ogre or a dinosaur.

Once you have all the parts you need, you can begin moving, scaling, and rotating biped parts to fit the mesh. It's a good idea to do all of this *before* you begin animating, because it will save you time in the long run. For example, if your character has short arms and large hands, it's much easier to tell whether the animation is correct if the biped also has short arms and large hands. If you were to animate first and pose later, you might find that the hands pass through the body during some parts of the animation, or that the swing of the arms doesn't look right with the new hands.

Setting Biped Parameters

Biped parameters indicate the body parts that will make up the biped unit, and also set the number of individual bones that will make up each body part. For example, if the biped has a long, flexible neck, you'll want to add more Neck links. Biped parameters also allow you to set the number of toes and fingers.

Immediately after you create the biped, you can change the biped parameters in the Create Biped rollout to make the biped more closely resemble your mesh. If you click anywhere in a viewport after creating the biped, you'll have to go to the Motion panel to change the biped structure. On the ⊚ Motion panel, turn on 🙂 Figure mode, and adjust the biped with the settings in the Structure rollout.

As you learn to pose the biped, experiment with the various options to see how they work. Try to use the built-in biped parts as much as possible. This will keep the biped operating as a single unit that you can easily manipulate. Although you can add custom Bones to the biped, the Biped tools create animation automatically only for biped parts, not for any Bones or other objects added to the biped.

On the Structure rollout, you can switch among four basic types of bipeds with the Body Type pull-down menu. The default type is Skeleton, which works well for most humanoid models. The Classic type was the only skeleton available in some earlier versions of Character Studio. The purpose of the Male and Female types is to help you visualize the animation better for a distinctly male or female model. The type of the biped has no effect on how easy or difficult it will be to pose the biped to a particular model.

▶QUICKLIST◀

CREATING A BIPED

❑ Make the biped about the same height as the mesh.

❑ Adjust the biped settings to match your mesh.

❑ Make a named selection set for the biped.

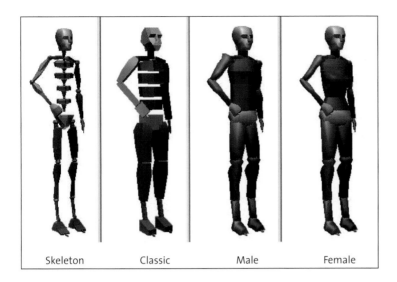

| Skeleton | Classic | Male | Female |

Most of the biped parameters are self-explanatory, but a few are less obvious, and some can be used in various ways. For example:

▶TIP◀

The choice of body type won't affect your animation; it's largely a matter of personal preference.

- Fingers include the thumb, as you'd expect. But the number of Fingers can be set to 0, while the number of Toes must be at least 1.

- Leg links actually comprise both the leg and foot. Leg Links set at 3 gives you a normal human leg with a thigh, calf, and foot; set at 4, you get a backward-bending leg like that of a bird. The extra bone between the calf and the foot is called a *horse link* in 3ds Max.

- Tail links stick out the back of the biped's pelvis, and can be used for any kind of tail. You can have up to 25 links in the tail.

- Ponytail1 and Ponytail2 links can be used for other protrusions from the head: not just hair, but a hat, a long dinosaur jaw, or dragon horns. (You'll get a chance to use Tail and Ponytail links in Section Three of this book.)

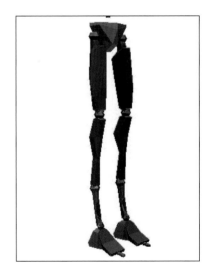

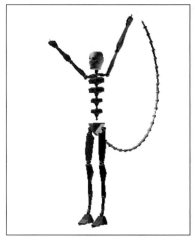

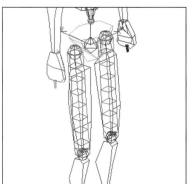

- Twist links are extra bones that can be used to counteract twisting that occurs in your mesh, particularly when the hands and feet are rotated. You turn them on and then choose which parts of the biped structure will have Twist links—you can have up to 10 for the upper arm, forearm, thigh, calf, and horse links. Twist links are frozen when they're created, and you unfreeze them to rotate them when needed.

- Props are stick-shaped links that attach to the biped's hands. Props are used primarily with motion capture data that includes a weapon wielded by a character.

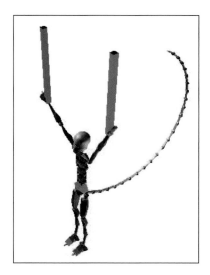

Finally, after choosing a type and setting parameters, you'll want to create a named selection set for the biped. This will make it easy to select the biped when you're working with 3ds Max. Select the entire biped, and enter the name in the Named Selection Set entry field on the toolbar. For our example in this chapter, use the name Biped.

Fitting the Biped to the Mesh

Once the biped has been created, you have to rotate and resize body parts to make the biped fit the mesh. This is done so that when the biped is associated with the mesh later on, each biped part will be associated with the appropriate part of the mesh.

Caution: When you're fitting the biped to the mesh, Figure mode must be turned on. This tells Character Studio that you are posing the biped (as opposed to animating it). This is extremely important. Don't forget to do this, or you'll suffer the frustration of spending perhaps hours posing a biped only to find that all your work was wasted.

To turn on Figure mode, click ![figure icon] Figure Mode on the ![motion icon] Motion panel. Then you can start moving and rotating the biped body parts to fit the mesh.

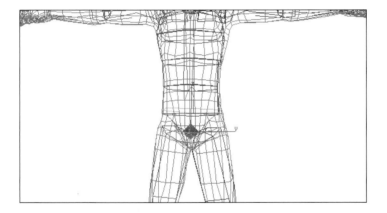

The first step is to move the entire biped body so it sits inside the mesh, by moving the biped's center of mass (COM). After the COM is placed, you can rotate and scale biped body parts to fit the mesh. Many body parts can be moved directly, but some parts can only be rotated.

Body parts should be centered inside their corresponding mesh parts as much as possible. Character Studio works best when the width of each part is resized to about three-quarters of the mesh width at that point.

When you begin rotating body parts, Character Studio automatically changes the coordinate system to Local. Ordinarily, 3ds Max will not change the coordinate system on its own, but because Local is actually the best coordinate system to use when rotating body joints, Character Studio does it automatically. The Local coordinate system allows you to rotate body parts more intuitively than other coordinate systems.

The next step in fitting the biped is to rotate the legs into position using the 3ds Max ⟳ Select and Rotate tool.

If the legs won't go into position, you'll have to scale the pelvis (an orange box appears around the COM). Never scale the center of mass—only the pelvis. If you scale the pelvis on its local Z axis, the legs can be rotated into position.

> **►TIP◄**
>
> Select one leg and then click 🧍 Symmetrical on the Track Selection rollout. The opposite leg will be added to the selection set. This is an easy way to rotate and scale limbs equally.

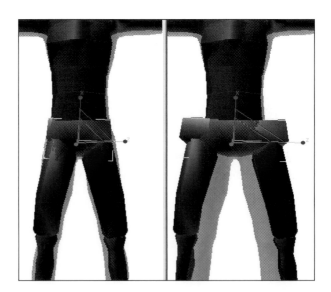

Most likely, the character will be posed with its arms spread outward. When fitting the arms, you'll have to rotate them upward to fit inside the mesh's arms. Usually, they'll be too high or too low, so you'll have to scale the Spine links up or down.

The *clavicles* are important arm bones because they control the shoulder area. This part can be rotated a little to fit the mesh, but not too much or you'll end up with very low or very high shoulders when the biped is animated.

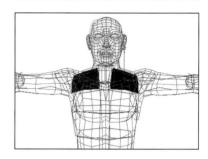

In order for Character Studio to work correctly in later steps, you have to give extra attention to the biped's extremities—its fingers, head, and toes. They must be scaled so they completely encompass the mesh's corresponding body parts. The adjacent figure shows the correct scaling for the biped feet in relation to the mesh.

Fitting the fingers to the mesh's fingers is often the most time consuming part of posing the biped. You can move the base of each finger, but the rest of the parts—each finger joint—must be rotated into place.

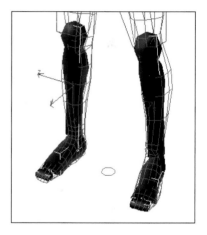

If the biped's fingers and hands will simply move along with the rest of the body, you can fudge this step a little and it will take less time. But if the biped will perform detailed finger movements (for example, playing the piano or doing woodworking), you'll have to work extensively in the Top, Front, and Left viewports to get the fingers positioned correctly. However, you can save time by posing one hand, and then use ⧉ Copy Posture and 🖫 Paste Posture Opposite to copy the pose to the other hand. (In 3ds Max 8 you have to click Create Collection before you can use Copy and Paste Posture.)

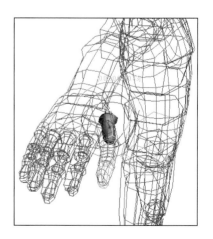

Fitting a Biped to a Mesh

In this exercise, you'll fit a biped to a gymnast model. This part of the Character Studio process usually takes a lot of time, even for experienced users. Go slowly and make sure you do each step correctly before going on to the next one. Position all body parts as close as possible to the center of the mesh's corresponding part.

Create the Biped

1. Load the file gymnast_mesh01.max from the CD that comes with this book.

   This scene contains an acrobat model that has been rotated to face the Front viewport and is ready for a biped. The model has been frozen so that you won't select it accidentally.

2. Go to the Create panel, click Systems, and click Biped. On the Create Biped rollout, set the Fingers value to 5 and the Finger Links to 3. Drag in the Front viewport to create a biped about the same height as the mesh.

Position the Center of Mass

1. Select any part of the biped, and go to the Motion panel.

2. Click the Figure Mode button to turn on Figure mode.

3. On the Track Selection rollout, click Body Horizontal to select the COM.

4. In the Front viewport, move the COM sideways to the pelvic area of the mesh.

   Don't be concerned if the arms and legs don't match up. Just get the center of mass into the right position.

▶TIP◀

When shaping the biped, learn to ignore the Perspective viewport. Your biped will go through a lot of changes before it is completely posed, so leave the Perspective viewport alone until the biped looks good in all the other viewports.

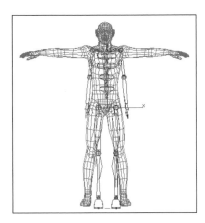

5. Click ⬍ Body Vertical, and move the COM up or down to position it correctly.

    Check both the Front and Left viewports to be sure the center of mass is right smack inside the pelvic area of the mesh, and move it as necessary.

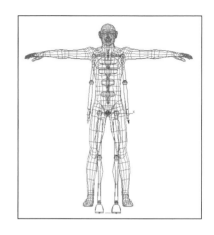

Position the Biped's Legs

Next, you'll position the biped's legs.

1. Select one of the biped's thighs.

2. Turn off the ⬔ Angle Snap Toggle if it's on, and click ↻ Select and Rotate.

    Notice that the coordinate system has changed to Local. If for some reason it doesn't change to Local, change it yourself.

    Also, make sure 🔳 Use Pivot Point Center is active—select it from the flyout if it's set to something else.

3. Rotate the thigh, trying to get the biped leg to go right down through the centers of the mesh leg.

4. If the biped legs don't fit inside the mesh, scale the pelvis on its local Z axis.

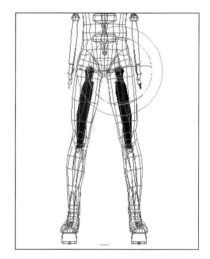

5. Work back and forth between scaling the pelvis and rotating the thighs until the biped legs go right through the mesh legs.

Fit the Legs

Now you'll work further on the legs in the Left viewport to fit them in the mesh. First you'll work on one leg, and then copy that leg's rotation and size to the other side of the biped. You can start with either leg.

1. In the Left viewport, select one thigh, and scale and rotate it so that the knee falls at the right spot on the mesh.

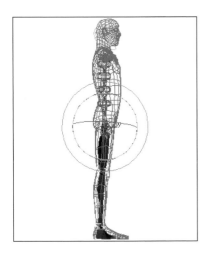

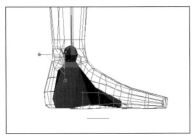

2. Do the same for the calf, so that the ankle falls at the right spot on the mesh. Note that you can't freely rotate the calf as you can the thigh, so you may have to revisit the thigh rotation to get the calf within the leg.

3. Check your work in the Front viewport and make sure the leg still looks right.

4. Scale the height of the foot to match the bottom of the mesh's foot.

   The biped toes will fall into the wrong place, but leave them as they are for now. You'll handle this in a separate step later on.

5. Select the thigh, calf, and foot that you just worked with. On the Copy/Paste rollout in the Copy Collections group, click the [icon] Create Collection button.

6. Click [icon] Copy Posture and then click [icon] Paste Posture Opposite. The changes to the leg are copied to the other leg.

   The newly posed leg should fit perfectly into the mesh. If it doesn't, you might need to move the center of mass a little to center it better on the mesh.

Adjust the Arm and Spine

Next, you'll position one arm and the spine. Do one arm first; later, you'll copy the position to the other arm. You'll need to work with both the spine and the arm in order to fit the arm to the mesh.

1. Select the upper part of one arm. In the Front viewport, rotate the arm until it's parallel to the mesh's arm.

   Don't be concerned if the biped arm doesn't fall exactly inside the mesh's arm.

2. Rotate the clavicle a little so that it points right at the armhole.

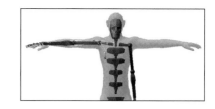

3. Select all Spine links, and make a named selection set called Spine.

   This will make it easier to select the spine again if necessary.

4. Scale the height of the spine to make the arm fall into place.

5. Scale the length of the clavicle so that its end just reaches the arm opening.

6. Check the Top and Left viewports, and rotate and scale the upper and lower arm to make the elbow and wrist fall into the right place. You may need to rotate some spine links to position the arms correctly.

Scale the Biped Parts

1. Scale the width of each spine link to just slightly less than the width of the mesh. Rescale the clavicle to compensate for the new width.

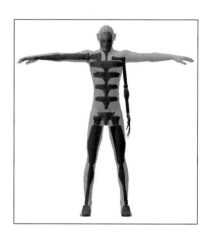

2. Scale the widths and depths of the upper and lower arm to slightly less than the size of the mesh.

3. Scale the thigh's width so it's slightly smaller of the width of the mesh at that spot. Do the same for the calf, and for the other leg as well.

4. Scale the hand to about the size of the mesh's palm.

Pose the Fingers

Next, you'll pose the fingers. Since our biped won't be doing any detailed finger movements, we can take the easy way out and just roughly pose them.

1. In the Top viewport, zoom in on the hand of the arm you've been working with.

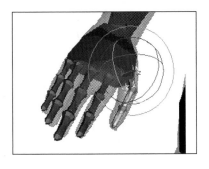

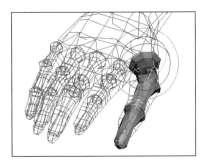

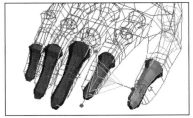

2. Move the base of each finger joint to the base of the corresponding finger on the mesh.

3. Rotate the base of each finger so that it matches the direction of the finger.

   As you rotate the biped fingers, you might find that the finger base has to be moved again in order to make the finger fall inside the mesh finger.

4. In the Top viewport, scale the width of each finger joint to slightly smaller than the width of the mesh's fingers.

5. Scale each finger joint so that the last joint extends beyond the mesh fingers. This will ensure that the finger envelopes will be created correctly.

6. In the Front viewport, rotate the finger joints so they roughly match the direction of the mesh's fingers. You can also scale the fingers to a thicker size. Be sure to move and rotate the thumb joints as well as the fingers.

7. Select the clavicle, upper arm, lower arm, hand, and fingers that you just worked with. Click ⊡ Copy Posture and then click ▣ Paste Posture Opposite.

   The arm posture has been copied to the opposite arm.

8. Exit Figure mode and save your file as Gymnast_mesh02.max.

   You've been working for a while on this project—it's good to save frequently when you've invested time on a file.

Pose the Head

As with the feet, we'll make the head extra large, so we've left it for the end. It makes it easier to see what's going on with the biped if you don't have these big clunky hands and feet and head hanging around.

1. Turn on Figure mode again then scale the neck upward so that the bottom of the biped head reaches the mesh's chin area.

2. Scale the biped head in both the Front and Left viewports to make it completely encompass the mesh's head.

3. Scale the neck width and depth so it's slightly smaller than the mesh.

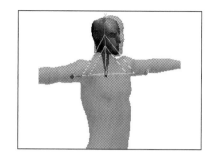

Pose the Feet

Now we'll take a look at the feet. There is another practical reason to leave the feet for last. You often end up fiddling with the arms and legs a lot to get them to fit right, so we leave the hands and feet for the end. The gymnast is wearing shoes, so we really don't need all those Toe links.

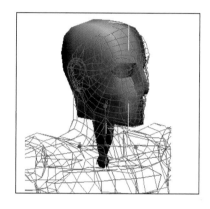

1. On the Motion panel, expand the Structure rollout.

2. If your biped has more than one toe, change Toes to 1, and change Toe Links to 1.

   Now you only have to deal with one toe on each foot.

3. In the Left viewport, scale the size of one toe to about one-quarter the length of the foot, and to the same height as the foot. In the Top viewport, scale the toe to the same width as the foot.

4. In the Top viewport, rotate the foot to match the direction of the mesh foot. Scale its length to extend just beyond the mesh foot.

5. Scale the height of the toe to cover the entire tip of the shoe.

> ►TIP◄
>
> Whenever possible, use the minimum number of fingers and toes. Also try to use the minimum number of Finger links and Toe links. For a character that's wearing shoes, you can simplify the animation process by giving the biped only one toe and one Toe link, and then resize that one toe to make it resemble a shoe.

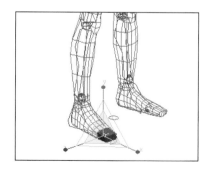

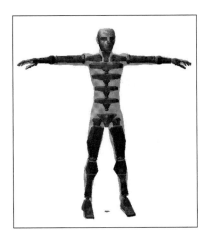

►NOTE◄

Character Studio can save all the Figure mode data about a biped in a FIG file. A FIG file stores the size of the biped, its structure, and its pose in Figure mode. The FIG file can then be loaded onto another biped to get the exact same pose again. This feature is handy for posing two or more bipeds with similar or identical bone structures. To create a FIG file, go into Figure mode and click Save File on the Biped rollout. To load a FIG file onto a biped, click Load File while in Figure mode.

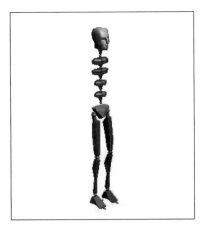

6. Copy and paste the foot and toe postures to the other side of the biped body.

   The entire body is now posed.

7. Exit Figure mode and save the file as `Gymnast_mesh03.max`.

Nonhuman Bipeds

So far, you've seen how to create a biped only for a humanoid character. Now you'll learn how to create bipeds for other types of characters, such as objects, animals with tails, and quadrupeds.

The concepts used for humanoid characters also apply to the other types. Follow the same sequence in posing the biped, applying skin, and testing the envelope assignment. However, there are additional rules for nonhumanoid characters to make them work properly with Character Studio.

First we'll go over a few of the options that really only apply to nonhumanoid characters, and then you'll get a chance to create a biped for an animal character.

Turn off the Arms checkbox to create a biped with no arms. This simplifies your work when you're animating objects like televisions, cash registers, and other items that have no discernible arms. As long as you want them to move like two-legged characters, Character Studio can handle them.

You'll need to add Neck links and Tail links for a dinosaur- or bird-type character that's bent over in its rest pose. For long necks and tails, use up to the maximum number (25) of Neck links and Tail links. By default, Tail links sit against the body and point straight down, but the base Tail link can be moved in any direction, and all Tail links can be rotated.

You can also use Ponytail1 and Ponytail2 links for the animal's jaw. By default these links are placed on top of the biped's head, but the base Ponytail link can be moved anywhere, and all Ponytail links can be rotated in any way. Here is an example of a animal jaw created with ponytail links.

EXERCISE 2.2

Biped for Quadruped Character

In this exercise, you'll create and pose a biped for a four-legged creature: a dog. For now, you'll simply create the biped and set its parameters. Because the biped is created standing up, it won't look much like a dog until you pose it in Exercise 2.3.

►TIP◄

You'd probably want to give this arm-less type of biped a wide stance to accommodate the object. The wide stance is achieved by scaling the pelvis horizontally.

1. Load the file DOG_MESH.MAX from the CD.

2. Select the entire mesh. Make sure all body parts are selected, and not just the body itself.

3. Create a named selection set called MESH.

4. Right-click and choose Properties, make the mesh See-Through, and freeze the mesh.

5. Create a biped standing next to the dog.

   Make it about twice the height of the dog. You'll scale the biped's spine and other parts when you pose it, so the height doesn't have to be exact.

6. Set the following parameters for the biped:

Neck Links	5
Leg Links	3
Tail Links	6
Ponytail1 Links	3

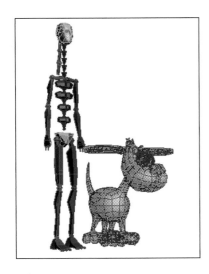

Ponytail2 Links	3
Fingers	3
Finger Links	1
Toes	3
Toe Links	2

7. Save the scene in your folder as DOG_MESH_BIPED.max.

Fitting a Nonhuman Biped to a Mesh

A biped is posed for a quadruped in the same way as for a two-legged character. Don't rotate the COM—just rotate and move the lowest Spine link to the correct location. Scale the arms and legs to fit the mesh, and pose any tail and Ponytail links appropriately.

In the adjacent figure, notice that the biped's head is facing straight ahead. If the mesh head is facing straight ahead, then so should the biped head. This rule is not so important if you plan to use only freeform animation. However, if you'll be using footsteps, you must pose the biped with the head facing forward. Otherwise, the biped head will snap back to its forward position when keys are created for footsteps, taking the mesh with it.

EXERCISE 2.3

Fit a Biped to a Dog Mesh

In this exercise, you'll fit the biped you made in Exercise 2.2 to the dog mesh.

1. Load the file DOG_MESH_BIPED.max that you created earlier, or load it from the CD.

2. Select a biped part, and go to the Motion panel.

3. Click ⚟ Figure Mode to turn it on.

4. Use ↔ Body Horizontal and ↕ Body Vertical to move the COM into the center of the dog's groin area. Check all viewports to make sure the COM is in the right place.

5. Rotate the legs into place. Work with both legs by first selecting one, then choosing ⬚ Symmetrical. Go up and down the leg parts' hierarchy by using the Page Up and Page Down keys.

   This step is a little tricky because the dog's legs bend outward a little bit. In addition, the third link behaves differently from the first two, as you'll see as soon as you try to move or rotate it. Just work on various parts of the leg until it fits correctly. Be sure to check all your viewports to make sure both legs are positioned just right.

6. Continue to refine the COM placement and the pelvis scaling until the leg fits. Scale the thighs, then the lower legs, and finally the feet.

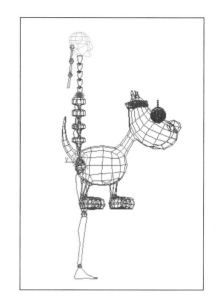

Position the Arms and Spine

1. Select all the Spine links, and make a named selection set called Spine.

2. Move and rotate the base Spine link so that it points along the center of the dog body.

3. Scale the spine links to fit the dog body.

4. Rotate one of the arms until it's parallel to the dog mesh foreleg. Scale the spine lengthwise so that the arm falls in the right place.

5. Scale the upper and lower arms to make the elbow and wrist fall in the right places.

6. Rotate the palms so that they face the ground.

7. Move and rotate the fingers into position to match the mesh's toes.

   This is another tricky step. You'll need to use the User view to see how the fingers are shaping up. Zoom in and rotate the view as much as necessary to get the fingers into the right spots.

8. Scale the biped components so the width and depth is slightly smaller than the mesh.

9. Copy and paste the arm position to the other arm.

Position the Neck and Head

1. Rotate and scale the neck pieces so that they go up the center of the neck. Scale the neck pieces to make the bottom of the biped head fall just about at the bottom of the mesh's head.

2. Scale the head's height to be a little taller than the mesh's head.

3. Move and rotate the Ponytail links so that they fall inside the ears. Scale the Ponytail links to get the ends extending beyond the ends of the ears. Scale the links' width so it is correct as well.

   This satisfies the rule for biped parts to extend beyond extremities.

4. Convert the biped head to an editable mesh. Move the vertices in the head object to better resemble the dog head.

Position the Tail and Feet

1. Move and scale the Tail links to fall inside the tail.

   The tail is also an extremity, so make sure the last Tail link extends beyond the end of the tail.

2. If necessary make adjustments to the scale of the feet to be about the same size as the mesh's feet.

3. Move the toes upward to form the paw. Scale and rotate the toes so that the bottom of the Toe links go through the center of the paw.

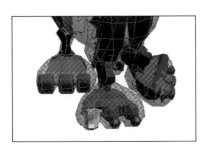

4. Scale the remaining toes to fit the dog's toes.

5. Scale each biped body part to slightly smaller than the mesh's width.

6. Save your work as DOG_MESH_BIPED02.MAX.

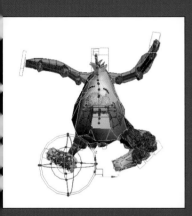

CHAPTER 3

Skinning

In order for the biped's animation to move your character, you
have to associate the character mesh with the biped's skeletal
parts. This is accomplished through a process called *skinning*.
Just as our own skin is moved by the motion of our bones and
muscles, your mesh character is animated by means of a skinning modifier that deforms the mesh according to the rotation
and position of the objects in the biped hierarchy. 3ds Max 8
comes with two modifiers that can be used for this purpose: the
Physique modifier and the Skin modifier.

►QUICKLIST◄

ASSOCIATING BIPED AND MESH

1. Make sure Figure mode is activated *before* applying the Skin or Physique modifier.

2. Apply Skin or Physique to all parts of the mesh, not just the main body.

3a. If you're using Skin, click the Add Bones button to add the biped objects to the list. Avoid adding the root Bip01 object, or any Bip footsteps that appear in the list.

3b. If you're using Physique, click Attach to Node and then click the Pelvis object, *not* the COM (Bip01).

Associating the Mesh

So far, you've made a biped and fitted it inside the mesh. But if you animate the biped as it is, it will simply walk away and leave the mesh behind. To make the biped control the mesh and move it around, you have to associate the biped with the mesh.

After the biped is correctly associated with the mesh (*skinned*), each part of the biped acts just like a bone inside a body. For example, when the lower arm bone moves, the lower arm portion of the mesh moves with it. In this way, each part of the biped acts as a bone. The biped is, in effect, a collection of bones linked together automatically to save you work.

At the time the mesh is skinned, vertices on the mesh are associated with one or more bones via a *weighting* system. A capsule-shaped envelope is created around each bone based on the bone's size. Vertices that fall within a bone's envelope receive some weight from it, meaning they are moved by it. A vertex that falls within the capsules of more than one bone receives appropriate weights from each bone.

In this chapter, we'll be using only the Skin modifier. But first let's take a brief look at the history of its predecessor, the Physique modifier. Originally, the whole Character Studio plug-in had to be purchased separately. When the Physique modifier was first released in 1995, it was a very sophisticated and ambitious program that allowed you to control the biped's influence on the mesh. Physique has controls for including and excluding vertices from bones; a means to create muscle bulges in arms and legs according to the angles between bones; and "tendons" that extend the influence of the bones to other parts of the biped.

Professional animators complained that they needed a skinning mechanism within 3ds Max—one they didn't have to pay extra for. So the Skin modifier was created and delivered for free as part of the 3ds Max software. At first it lacked some of the sophisticated features of Physique, but over time it has continued to improve. Meanwhile, development has stopped on Physique. Like

Biped, Physique is now included with 3ds Max and is essentially the same software that originally shipped, with a few bugs fixed.

In addition to skinning, the Skin modifier also allows the deformation of character-mesh objects by associating the bones with mesh vertices. This is done using the capsule-shaped envelopes, which control specific vertices.

The Skin modifier also includes the ability to define bulges based on the angles between bones. However, unlike Physique, Skin allows you to mirror the bone-vertex assignments from one side of the body to the other.

Skin Morph and Skin Wrap

The Skin Morph and Skin Wrap modifiers have been included with 3ds Max since version 7. Skin Morph allows you to fine-tune the way vertices respond, based on the angles between bones. It provides a more controlled method for creating muscle bulges, and for keeping elbows and knees from crimping when the angle between the bones is very sharp.

The Skin Wrap modifier expands on the Skin modifier, so that you're not limited to having bones drive the animation. Skin Wrap lets you use the vertex movement of a low-poly mesh to drive the animation of a high-poly character, for example. This means you can set up the animation with a low-poly mesh and fine-tune it with a faster playback speed before switching to the high-poly mesh for the final rendering.

Another use for Skin Wrap is to employ spline objects to drive the animation of a mesh. For example, you could animate a spline's vertices to mimic a wagging-tail motion, and then use Skin Wrap to make a mesh follow this motion.

Skin Wrap works at either the vertex- or face-deformation level. It offers a Mirror mode, just as the Skin modifier does. You can also "bake" the animation into the vertices so that the mesh retains its deformation independently of the controlling mesh or spline.

Preparing to Use Skin

Before applying Skin to a mesh, make sure the bones fit nicely inside the geometry. The initial envelopes, and thus the vertex weights, depend on the size and orientation of the bones. If the bones inside the mesh are too skinny, the envelopes will be too small, and the vertices will not become weighted to any of the bones.

Both Physique and Skin are best applied to objects rather than groups. If your objects have been grouped, we recommend that you ungroup them before applying Physique or Skin. In fact, for any character animation it's wise to make your own hierarchies and avoid the use of groups entirely, whenever possible.

Each weighting envelope is a capsule with an inner and outer gizmo. The vertices within the inner gizmo are completely affected by the movement of the bone. The vertices between the inner and outer bounds are *weighted,* or somewhat affected by the bone movement. The vertices that fall outside the gizmos are not at all affected by the bone movement.

You need to adjust each envelope so that it only affects the required portion of the mesh. You don't want the movement of the head, for example, to influence the arms or even the shoulders. You can do this initially when you associate the biped and mesh, but you'll also need to revisit each envelope after creating a test animation that shows you how the bone movement is influencing the mesh.

The general workflow of skin vertex weighting is to go through the bone envelopes and adjust the radius of each end of the capsules, as well as reposition the capsule ends to fit within the length of the biped skeletal bones. At this time you can also add additional cross sections to the envelopes to allow for finer control. Occasionally you will need to rotate the envelopes if they have been incorrectly oriented. This happens when the bones are wider than they are long.

In 3ds Max 8 there is a new command in the Skin modifier called Weight All Vertices. This command is turned on by default, and it ensures that every vertex in the mesh will be assigned to at least one bone object. In previous versions of the software, some vertices in the toes or fingers very commonly remained unassigned, requiring manual assignment to some bone. So keep Weight All Vertices turned on and you'll save yourself a lot of work; look for it near the bottom of the Advanced Parameters rollout.

EXERCISE 3.1

Associating Biped and Mesh

In this exercise, you'll associate a biped and its fitted mesh, and then check the envelopes for correct size and orientation.

1. Load the file `Rabbit_start_skin.max` from the CD. Here you can see a rabbit mesh in the typical DaVinci pose, with arms spread out horizontally away from the sides of the body and feet slightly apart as well.

2. Select the mesh then right-click and choose Properties to open the Object Properties dialog. In the Display Properties group, turn on See-Through and then click OK.

    Now the mesh is transparent. The biped is still hidden.

3. Right-click again and choose Unhide All from the right-click quad menu.

    Now you can see the biped within the rabbit mesh.

4. Select any part of the biped and go to the Motion panel.

5. On the Biped rollout, turn on 🚶 Figure mode.

    Notice that no change occurs in this mesh. The rabbit biped hasn't been animated in this file. (Often the biped will jump to a new location when Figure mode is turned on.)

6. Select the mesh of the rabbit. The object is named `rabbit_lr`.

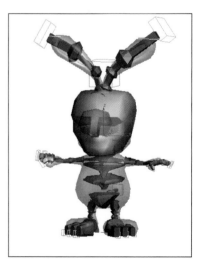

7. On the Modify panel, click the drop-down arrow for the Modifier list and choose Skin. This adds the modifier to the mesh object.

8. To add the biped objects as bones, go to the Parameters rollout. In the Bones group, click Add.

9. On the list that appears, click All. Holding down Ctrl, click the Bipo1 root object to remove it from the list. Then click Select.

10. In the Parameters rollout, click Edit Envelopes.

    Bipo1 Tail (at the bottom of the list) is selected and its envelope highlighted in the viewport.

11. In the list, highlight each biped object to display its envelope in the viewport. Notice that some envelopes are relatively small, and some are very large.

12. Save your file as Rabbit_skin.max.

Working with the Test Animation

After your initial pass at the envelopes, you can create a test animation for the biped and review the envelope performance. You'll inevitably find vertices, usually in the hands and feet, that are not assigned or are incorrectly assigned. You can then do manual weighting of the vertices using the 3ds Max 8 Weight Tool to quickly adjust the vertex and bone association.

Create any kind of test animation you like, based on the animation required for your character. If the character is going to be walking, you can use the Footstep animation method is create a fast walk cycle for skinning purposes. If, however, your character needs to raise its hands above its head or do the splits, then you'll want to create this kind of animation manually using Freeform mode. Or you can also just load in any BIP file to accomplish this motion testing. The footstep motion serves to help you see how the skinning deforms the mesh, any other BIP file with sufficient motion will do the same thing.

EXERCISE 3.2

Setting Up a Test Walk

In this exercise you'll set up a walk for use in testing the skinning of the rabbit biped.

1. Use the file you've been working on, or load `Rabbit_skin.max` from the CD that comes with the book.

2. Press the h key and select the rabbit_lr object. Right-click and choose Properties, and turn off See-Through. Then, in the right-click quad menu, click Hide Selection to hide the display of the rabbit mesh in the viewport.

3. Select any part of the biped.

4. Go to the ⊚ Motion panel.

5. If necessary, turn off ⚐ Figure mode and turn on 👣 Footstep mode.

6. On the Footstep Creation rollout, click ⊞ Create Multiple Footsteps.

   The Create Multiple Footsteps dialog appears.

   In later chapters we'll examine the options in this dialog. For now, we'll just create a few footsteps.

7. Change Number of Footsteps to 8; then click OK to exit the dialog and create the footsteps.

   The rabbit has large feet, and the footsteps are quite close together. You can scale the footsteps to better suit this rabbit.

8. In the Footstep Operations rollout, use the Scale spinner to lengthen and widen the footsteps.

9. Click ⊞ Create Keys for Inactive Footsteps.

10. Play the animation. The biped walks.

►QUICKLIST◄

TEST FOOSTEPS

1. Make sure you're out of Figure mode.

2. Click Footstep Mode to access the footstep creation tools.

3. Click Create Multiple Footsteps to create footstep icons automatically.

4. Click Create Keys for Inactive Footsteps to make the biped move through the footsteps.

11. Hide everything in the scene. Then unhide just the rabbit and play the animation again. Now you can see that the skin modifier is driving the animation of the rabbit mesh using the biped's bones.

12. Look for unnatural stretching as the character moves. In our rabbit, check the legs and the feet; they may be influenced by the envelopes from the spine. Be sure to review the animation from several different views—you'll be surprised what you find when you look at it from the side, back, or from underneath.

This rabbit is a round and fat character, and his belly and love handles collide with the arms during the animation. The arms in fact pass through the sides of the rabbit's hips. This is the fault of the animation, not the skinning.

13. Exit Footstep mode. If you want to see a freeform animation instead of using footsteps, unhide the biped and select any biped part. Then in the Biped rollout of the Motion panel, choose 📂 Load File.

14. Find the `rabbit_test_animation.bip` file on the CD and load it in. The rabbit raises his toes and hangs from one paw.

In the adjacent illustration, we've hidden the biped.

Correcting Skin Problems

EXERCISE 3.3

Check the Deformation

The rabbit mesh in our test walk didn't exhibit any particular problems, so we'll use a different mesh this time. Once we've spotted any weighting problems, we can adjust the weights to make the mesh deform more correctly.

1. Open the file `DOG_MESH_BIPED_skin.max` and play the animation.

The dog stretches all four legs in different directions.

2. Navigate around the dog and you'll see that there is a problem with the front legs.

3. Go to frame 35 and arc-rotate around the dog.

   What's happening is that the left paw is being influenced by the movement of the right-front paw.

Adjusting Skin Envelopes

To correct this inappropriate influence, you can simply make adjustments to the offending envelope.

1. Select the dog mesh. Then in the Modify panel, turn on Edit Envelopes in the Parameters rollout.

2. Move the time slider back to frame 0.

3. Click on each of the bone envelopes in the list to observe the size and orientation of each skin envelope. Can you find the offending envelope?

   It's the skin envelope for Bipo1 R Finger2, which is bigger than it needs to be. Because it's wider than necessary, it's affecting some of the vertices that create the left front paw of the dog.

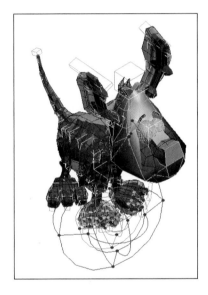

Changing the Radial Scale

To fix the weighting problem on Bipo1 R Finger2, you'll change the radial scale of the offending envelope.

You can change the size of an envelope's inner and outer gizmos by clicking in the viewport on the dots that lie on the gizmo. Selecting any dot will let you directly move all of them using the Transform gizmo in the viewport. Or you can achieve the same result by going to the Envelope Properties section of the Parameters rollout and changing the Radius spinner.

1. Go to frame 35, and select the dots on the right side of the `Bip01 R Finger2` envelope.

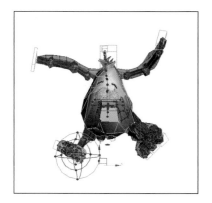

2. Use the Transform gizmo to decrease the radius. The envelope is now the correct size, but the vertices may still not return to their correct position.

   If the vertices in the opposite paw refuse to return to their correct position, there is another tool that will let you fix this problem.

3. In the Weight Properties section click the [icon] Weight Tool.

4. In the Parameters rollout, make sure Select Vertices is checked, then select the offending vertices in the viewport. The bones that influence those vertices will be displayed in a list in the Weight Tool window.

5. Locate the Bip01 R Finger2 bone in the list and select it, then change its weight to 0 by clicking the preset 0 button. The stubborn vertices will now respond.

Changing the Envelope Length

The length of the envelope can be changed just as the radial scale can be. Every envelope has a gizmo at the center of each ball end of the capsule. By selecting this point, you can lengthen or shorten the envelope easily.

1. Arc-rotate around the dog so you can see the back-left leg. With Edit Envelopes on select the Bip01 L Calf. (You can see that the envelope has been extended for this exercise.)

2. Use the Transform gizmo to move the capsule end and change the envelope length. In the screen capture shown here, we've moved the envelope end downward, so that you can clearly see the point you need to select, without obstruction from the mesh or other bone objects.

3. Reposition the end of the capsule to make the Bip01 L Calf envelope an appropriate length.

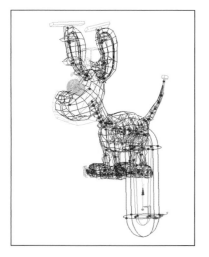

Rotating the Envelope

When a bone envelope is created, it is oriented to match its longest dimension. So a bone that's wider than it is long can result in a capsule that needs to be reoriented. You can use the same point selected for changing the envelope length, to reorient the capsule. Simply moving the capsule end in any axis other than the one that's the same as its length will result in the capsule's stretching and rotating at the same time.

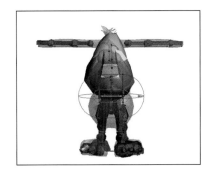

1. On the Parameters rollout, select `Bip01 Spine1` in the Bone list. This bone envelope that needs to be rotated.

2. Select one capsule end and move it outside the dog's body. Then move it downward until it's under the belly.

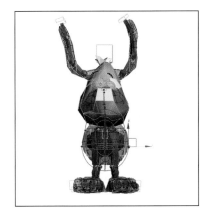

3. Select the other capsule end and move it so that the capsule is positioned vertically rather than horizontally. Reposition the capsule ends (using several views) until the capsule is as shown in the adjacent illustration.

   Capsules can be distorted by changing the radius of one end and leaving the other end alone. In this example, the dog's belly is fat and wide, and the capsule needs a large radius to accommodate the extra girth.

   Since this is 3D, it's a good idea to observe the same envelope from another view. Looking from the left, in the adjacent pair of pictures you can see the dog envelope as it was originally created, and then after it has been adjusted.

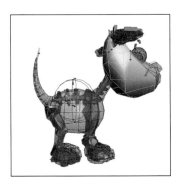

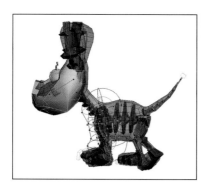

4. Select any point on the outer radius of the Spine1 envelope, and use the Transform gizmo to extend it. You want all the vertices within the belly to be influenced by the envelope.

Adding and Removing Cross Sections

You'll next refine the shape of the capsule by adding more cross sections to the envelope. In the Cross Sections area, just click the Add button, and then click in the envelope wherever you want to add the cross section.

1. Select the dog's Bipo1 L UpperArm bone.

2. In the Cross Sections area, click the Add button, and then click in the center of the envelope to add cross sections.

   Add three cross sections in the center. These additional cross sections will let you sculpt the shape of the envelope as necessary.

Mirror Mode

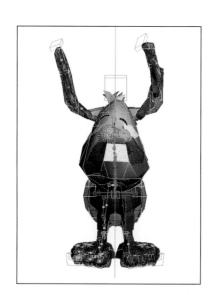

Mirror mode lets you establish a mirror plane and then mirror all the vertex weighting from one side of the biped to the other. You use the green/blue symmetry that's built into the Biped system for copying and pasting. Either paste from the green bones to the blue bones (and vice versa), or from the green vertices to the blue vertices. Pasting vertices gives you the fine control you'll need to perfect the skin weighting. Give it a try.

1. Select an envelope on the left side of the biped, and move it so that it's incorrect. For instance, select Bipo1 L Forearm and move it entirely outside the mesh of the dog.

2. In the Mirror Parameters rollout, turn on Mirror mode.

   The mirror plane appears. Arc-rotate around the dog to examine the placement of the mirror plane. In the adjacent illustration, you can see the mirror plane dividing the dog mesh into two halves.

3. Select all the green bones in the dog by dragging a selection rectangle in the viewport. The selected bones are highlighted in yellow.

4. In the Mirror Parameters rollout, click ⬚ Paste Green to Blue Bones.

5. Exit Mirror mode. Check the envelope you messed up; it's now corrected.

Adjusting the Head Envelope

The head envelope is often in need of adjustment. It often happens that your character mesh has a shape that is very different from the default biped mesh. If your character is a dog or dinosaur, for instance, it may have a long snout or extended jaws that don't match the humanoid head that the biped comes with.

You can collapse the Bip01 object to an editable poly or editable mesh object, and then reshape the head object to more closely resemble the character mesh. Still, you'll have to work on the head envelope to reorient and shape it to encompass the correct vertices. Use the same methods described in Exercise 3.3 to reorient and shape the envelope so that it surrounds the correct mesh vertices.

Vertex Weighting

Sometimes you need to control the vertex skin assignment at a finer level than by simply using the envelope controls. To do this, you can assign weighting to the vertices; the weighting indicates the influence the bone will have on the vertices. A weight of 0 means there is no influence; a weight of 1 means there is complete influence by that bone's movement over that vertex. 3ds Max 8 offers a fast Weight Tool that lets you select the vertices in the viewport and then quickly assign preset weights using the floating dialog. This makes it very easy to include or exclude troublesome vertices.

To use the new Weight Tool click the button with a picture of a wrench in the Weight Properties section. Then select the vertices and you will see all the bones that influence the selection. Select any bone in the list, then click the preset values to change the influences, or use the Set Weight spinner to get other values.

When multiple bones share influence on vertices, the multiple weights will always add up to 1.0. The Weight Tool helps you to see the bones that are in play and then quickly adjust the values for the weighting.

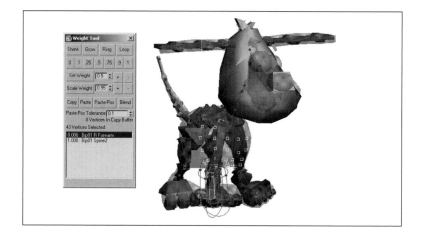

In the Weight Properties group of the Parameters rollout, you can also use the ⊗ Exclude Selected Vertices and ⊕ Include Selected Vertices buttons to affect the relationships of skin vertices and bone motion. If you like the weighting of the vertices, you can use the 🗇 Bake Selected Vertices button to "bake" the weights. If you do this, changing the bone envelope won't affect those vertices.

Weights can also be painted into the mesh. Use the Brush Presets to customize your paintbrush and then paint the weights directly onto the mesh in the viewport.

Copy and Paste Envelopes

Most characters are more or less symmetrical. As in nature, beings in the virtual environment appear to be designed along a central axis, with pairs of limbs and bones radiating from a core. You can save yourself a lot of tedious work by copying and pasting envelopes from one bone to another using the Copy and Paste buttons found in the Envelope Properties section. You can paste to one bone, or paste to all bones.

To see more than one bone envelope at once, turn on the Envelope Visibility button in the same section. Select the bone and click the button. The envelope will remain visible when you select the next bone. You can see as many envelopes as you like using this method.

Using ENV Files

It's easy to spend a full day adjusting the weights and envelopes of a character—and all this hard work can be saved into a skin envelope file with the extension .ENV. It's a good idea to do this, because you can then reload the .ENV file onto this biped if needed, or onto any other biped or skeleton made of Max bones. You'll find the Load and Save buttons for skin files in the Advanced Parameters rollout. Make a habit of saving the ENV file separately from your Max file.

If you try to load a skin file onto a character with differently named bones, you'll get a dialog that allows you to specify the copy-and-paste operation from bone to bone.

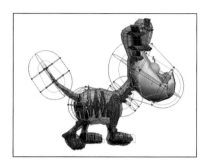

> **►TIP◄**
>
> Remembering to save a skin file can save you a lot of work. If you have to delete a skin modifier and then need to reapply it to a character, loading a skin file could save you perhaps hours of vertex weighting and envelope manipulation.

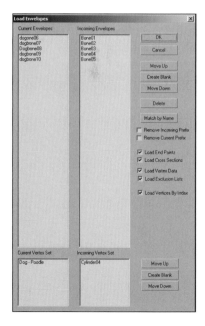

Footstep Animation

Placing Character Studio's footsteps icons in your scene makes your biped skeleton move from one footstep to the next.

For cartoon, game, or other types of animation, you can use footsteps as a quick way to get some action going with the biped. Many animators use footsteps as a starting point for their animation and then convert the footsteps to freeform mode so they can adjust the animation to their needs.

One great benefit of footsteps is that they force the biped's motions to follow natural laws of time and space. First, we'll look at the basic types of footsteps and how they make the biped move in different ways. Then we'll work on refining the timing of footsteps to make the motion smoother. We'll finish this section with the advanced footstep tools that let you adjust your biped's balance and timing very precisely.

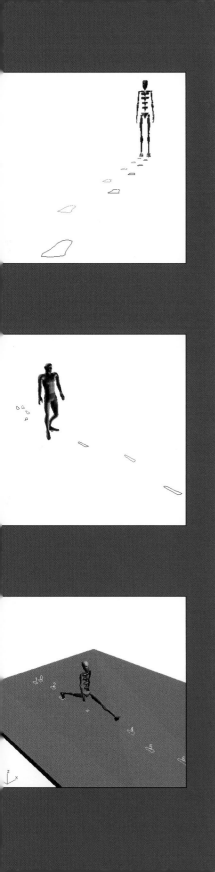

CHAPTER 4

Basic Footsteps

There are three basic types of auto footsteps: *Walk*, *Run*, and *Jump*. Each one causes your biped to move in a specific way from one footstep icon to the next.

We'll look at each of the footstep types and create some basic animations and then edit the placement of existing footsteps to add some variety.

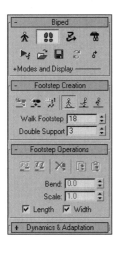

Gaits

All the footstep tools are accessed by selecting the biped, going to the Motion panel, and clicking ![icon] Footstep Mode. This displays a number of tools on the Footstep Creation and Footstep Operations rollouts.

The Walk, Run, and Jump buttons on the Footstep Creation rollout define the *gait*, or pattern of foot movement. When creating footsteps, you should first pick the type of gait that best approximates the movement you want.

The gait you choose affects both the placement and timing of footsteps. ![icon] Walk creates alternating footsteps with at least one foot down at all times, and the body is never completely in the air. The ![icon] Run gait also generates alternating footsteps, but the body is in the air between footsteps. The ![icon] Jump gait creates simultaneous footsteps for both feet, so either both feet are down or the body is in the air.

Each gait has two parameters that control how long each part of the gait will last. The default settings for these parameters will create medium-speed motion.

- Walk uses the *Walk Footstep* parameter to determine the length of time a foot is down, and *Double Support* to set the amount of time both feet are down.

- Run uses the *Run Footstep* parameter to set the length of time a foot is down, and *Airborne* to set the amount of time the entire body is in the air.

- Jump uses the *2 Feet Down* parameter to set the amount of time both feet are down, and *Airborne* to set the amount of time the body is in the air between landings.

Once you've chosen the basic gait, click ![icon] Create Multiple Footsteps to automatically generate several footsteps with the chosen gait. Before the footsteps appear in your scene, though, you'll see a Create Multiple Footsteps dialog. This is where you change the default values for your chosen gait.

This dialog focuses on values for stride length and width:

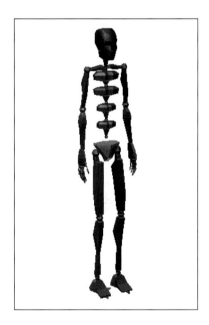

- The *stride length* is the distance that one foot travels. When you walk right-left-right-left, the stride length is the distance between two right footsteps or two left footsteps.

- The *stride width* is the distance between the feet, regardless of the stride length. A big, bumbling ogre has a wide stride width, and a mincing harlequin has a narrow stride width.

- Stride length and width can be *parametric* or *actual*. The parametric value sets the stride width as a percentage of the pelvis, and the stride length as a percentage of the length of the biped leg. The actual value uses the modeling units used in the scene.

EXERCISE 4.1

Footstep Practice

In this exercise, you'll practice working with the options in the Create Multiple Footsteps dialog.

1. Reset 3ds Max.

2. Create a biped of any size.

3. Save the file as MYBIPED.MAX in your folder.

4. Select any biped part and go to the ⊚ Motion panel.

5. Click 👣 Footstep Mode to turn it on.

6. Choose the 🚶 Walk gait if it's not already highlighted.

7. Click Create Multiple Footsteps.

8. In the General section of the Create Multiple Footsteps dialog, set Number of Footsteps to 12.

9. Change the Actual Stride Width to a slightly higher number than the default.

   This will make the biped's stride wider.

10. Click OK to exit the dialog.

    You've created 12 footsteps for the biped to follow.

Create Keys for Footsteps

1. Click 🔲 Create Keys for Inactive Footsteps.

2. Click the ▶ Play Animation button and watch the animation.

   Note how the biped moves through the footsteps. Its body is never entirely in the air. Note how long each foot stays on the ground.

3. Save the file as MYBIPEDWALK.MAX.

Try New Gaits

1. Load the file MYBIPED.MAX again.

2. Create another set of footsteps just as you did previously, this time choosing the 🔲 Run gait in the Footstep Creation rollout. Be sure to create keys for the footsteps after you create them. Play the animation.

   Note how the biped moves through the footsteps. Its body is entirely in the air during the airborne period. Note how long each foot stays on the ground. Note that the run cycle is much less convincing than the walk cycle. If you are trying to create a character running, you will need to do some serious work on this before it's believable.

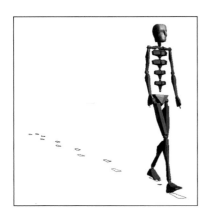

3. Load MYBIPED.MAX again and create another set of footsteps, this time with the 🔲 Jump gait.

4. Load MYBIPED.MAX again. Pick a gait, and make some changes to the parameters in the Create Multiple Footsteps dialog. Try changing the Actual Stride Height. Click Create Keys for Inactive Footsteps and watch the animation.

The biped climbs up into the air when the stride height is increased.

5. Continue reloading the file and trying different settings in the Create Multiple Footsteps dialog. Experiment with various stride lengths, widths, and heights.

   Keep trying out different gaits and parameters until you feel comfortable creating footsteps in a variety of ways using the Create Multiple Footsteps dialog.

Editing Footstep Placement

The footstep icons themselves can be moved and rotated to make the biped move around in different ways. When you're in Footstep mode, only footsteps can be selected. You select one or more footsteps as you would select any 3ds Max object—click a footstep in a viewport, or hold the Ctrl key and click to select multiple footsteps, or draw a selection region around the footsteps you want to select.

Once you've selected footsteps, you can use ⊕ Select and Move or ↻ Select and Rotate to transform the footsteps.

EXERCISE 4.2

Moving and Rotating Footsteps

This exercise gives you practice in moving and rotating footsteps. Here, you'll make the biped walk over a hill.

1. Load MYBIPEDWALK.MAX.

2. In the Top viewport, create a large box to represent the ground. The box should be big enough to include the biped and all the footsteps. Set the box's Length Segs and Width Segs to 15. Right-click the Perspective viewport label and choose Edged Faces so that you can see the segments.

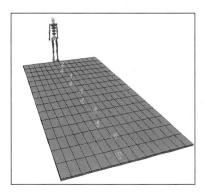

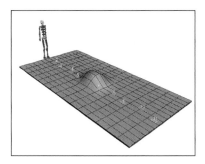

3. Move the box underneath the biped and apply the Affect Region modifier to the box.

   A bump in the ground forms about halfway along the biped's total walking path.

4. Expand the Affect Region modifier in the Modifier Stack, and select Points. Then select and adjust the Point gizmo in the viewport to change the bump height. When you're happy with the bump, turn off the Points for the Affect Region modifier.

   The Affect Region modifier will only work if you've given the box numerous Length Segs and Width Segs. You'll probably need to adjust the Falloff parameter for the Affect Region modifier in order to make the bump the right size.

Transforming the Footsteps

Next, you'll move and rotate the biped's footsteps so they follow the bump in the ground.

1. Select the biped and go to the ⊚ Motion panel.

2. Click 👣 Footstep Mode to turn it on.

3. Select the footstep nearest the bump, and move it so it sits above the bump.

4. For the rest of the footsteps, move and rotate them to follow the contours of the bump.

5. Click 👣 Create Keys for Inactive Footsteps; then click ▶ Play Animation.

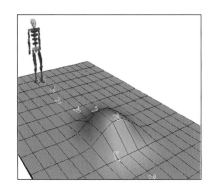

As the biped steps over the bump, one or both of its feet might pass through the bump at the top. You'll learn how to fix this problem in Chapter 5.

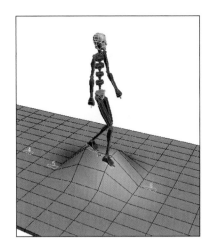

6. Save the scene in your folder with the filename BUMP.MAX.

You can also use the Bend and Scale values under the Footstep Operations rollout to bend or scale a group of footsteps. Select a set of footsteps; then change the Bend or Scale value. Bend and Scale change the relationships between footsteps, not the size or shape of the footsteps themselves. Footsteps are always the same size and shape as the biped foot.

EXERCISE 4.3

Walking in Circles

The Bend and Scale parameters provide a quick and easy way to move and rotate footsteps. In this exercise you'll practice using these two parameters.

1. Open the file Walk_in_circles.max from the CD.

2. Select any biped part and go to the ⊕ Motion panel.

3. Click 👣 Footstep Mode to turn it on.

    Leave the gait set to 🚶 Walk.

4. Click 👣 Create Multiple Footsteps. Set Number of Footsteps to 20, and click OK to exit the dialog.

    By default, all the footsteps are selected. Leave them selected.

5. Click Zoom Extents All to see the footsteps in all viewports.

6. On the Footstep Operations rollout, increase the Bend parameter to about 19.

    This makes the footsteps go in a circle. Note that after you enter a new value for Bend, it resets to 0.

►NOTE◄

After Bend and Scale are changed, they always reset themselves back to 0. This means Bend and Scale don't work like modifiers—you can't come back later and adjust an earlier bending or scaling operation.

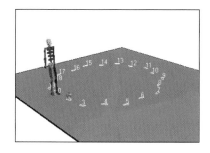

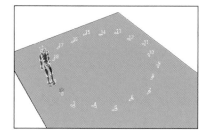

7. Click ⬚ Create Keys for Inactive Footsteps and then play the animation.

   The biped walks in a circle.

8. Save the scene in your folder with the filename CIRCLE.MAX.

Character Studio allows you to move footsteps anywhere in the 3ds Max world space, and the biped will endeavor to get its feet into the footsteps on time. If the footsteps are very far apart, the biped may be forced to do the splits or perform other contortions. A common error is to place the left and right footsteps in such a way that the biped has to cross its legs in a most uncomfortable fashion, sometimes actually moving one leg through the other to get to a footstep.

When first learning Character Studio, it can be fun and educational to experiment with wildly varying footstep placements just to see what will happen. But in the end, it's up to you to make sure your footstep placements make sense and result in a coherent animation.

EXERCISE 4.4

Biped Does the Splits

In this exercise, you'll move footsteps far apart, forcing the biped to go through crazy moves to get to the footsteps.

1. Reset 3ds Max, and create a biped of any size.

2. Select any biped part and go to the ⬚ Motion panel. Click ⬚ Footstep Mode to turn it on. Leave the gait set to ⬚ Walk.

3. Click ⬚ Create Multiple Footsteps. Set Number of Footsteps to 8, and click OK to exit the dialog.

   Next, you'll dramatically alter the placement of the footsteps.

4. In the Left viewport, select footsteps 4 through 7.

5. Move these footsteps to the right so they are some distance from footstep 3, as shown in the figure. This screenshot has an added box so you can see the footsteps more easily.

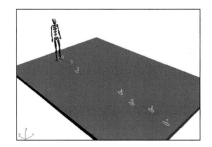

6. Click 🔲 Create Keys for Inactive Footsteps and play the animation.

   The biped does the splits as it attempts to do footstep 4 in the specified time. Ouch!

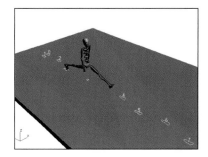

7. Save the scene with the filename SPLITS.MAX in your folder.

   This exercise has illustrated what happens when you place footsteps too far apart for the biped's natural movement. It still wants to get its foot into the footstep at the specified time, and will go through all manner of contortions to get there. If you want footsteps far apart, you'll have to adjust the timing, which you'll learn how to do in Chapter 5.

Footstep Sequences

You can use automatic footstep creation to create a series of different footstep types. For example, you could use the Walk gait to create 8 footsteps, and then change the gait to Run and click Create Multiple Footsteps again to create 12 more footsteps. You'd then have a total of 20 footsteps that start with a walk and turn into a run. You can create as many footsteps as you like in this manner.

EXERCISE 4.5

Footsteps for the Gymnast

In this exercise, you'll set up some footsteps for the gymnast.

1. Load gymnastic_strechings.max from the CD that comes with this book. This file contains the gymnast mesh to which Skin has been applied.

   ▶ Play the animation to see the gymnast stretch and then touch his toes.

2. Right-click in the Perspective viewport and choose Unhide All.

3. Select a biped body part and go to the ⊛ Motion panel.

   The first thing you'll do is delete the existing footsteps.

4. Click 👣 Footstep Mode and then draw a selection region around all the footsteps.

   Because you're in Footstep mode, only footsteps will be selected.

5. Click ✕ Delete Footsteps on the Footstep Operations rollout.

Create Consecutive Footsteps

Now you'll create footsteps for your own animation.

1. Use the 🗗 Create Multiple Footsteps dialog to create three footstep sequences. For each gait, click Create Multiple Footsteps, set the Number of Steps, and click OK. Create the footstep sequences in the following order:

   4 🚶 Walk footsteps

   4 🏃 Run footsteps

   8 🤸 Jump footsteps

   This creates a total of 16 footsteps in the scene.

2. Move and rotate some of the footsteps to customize the animation. You can also use Bend and Scale if you like.

   Take care not to move the footsteps too far apart, or the gymnast will become contorted when you create keys for the footsteps.

3. Click ⊡ Create Keys for Inactive Footsteps to activate the footsteps.

4. Hide the biped.

5. ▶ Play the animation.

6. Save the file as `gymnastic_footsteps.max` in your folder.

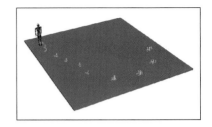

You can move or rotate footsteps after footstep keys have been created. However, this sometimes produces strange motion. There's a way to avoid this.

If you need to move or rotate footsteps after keys have been created, you should remove the keys and then regenerate them. To do this, select all the footsteps and click Deactivate Footsteps. Then click Create Keys for Inactive Footsteps again to regenerate keys for the footsteps based on their current locations and orientations.

EXERCISE 4.6

Adjusting Footsteps After Key Creation

In this exercise, you'll see firsthand what happens when footsteps are moved after keys are created. Then you'll practice fixing the footsteps.

1. Reset 3ds Max, and create a new biped of any size.

2. Select any biped part and go to the ⊚ Motion panel.

3. Click ⚇ Footstep Mode to turn it on. Set the gait to Walk.

4. Click ⊞ Create Multiple Footsteps. Set Number of Footsteps to 8 and click OK to exit the dialog.

5. Click ⊡ Create Keys for Inactive Footsteps.

6. In the Top viewport, move each footstep so it's under or very close to the biped.

7. Play the animation.

   The biped looks as if it's stamping its feet.

   To make the motion more natural, you'll deactivate the footsteps and then create keys for them again.

8. Select all the footsteps. Click ⧉ Deactivate Footsteps.

9. Click ⧉ Create Keys for Inactive Footsteps.

10. Play the animation.

   The biped now moves its legs naturally.

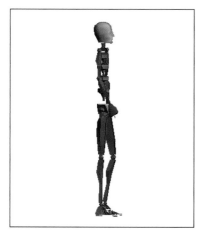

CHAPTER 5

Footstep Timing

It's important to distinguish between footstep *placement* and footstep *timing*. Footstep placement is the physical location of footsteps in the viewport. Footstep timing is the frame on which a footstep key starts and the number of frames it lasts, as determined by the gait and other parameters, such as 2 Feet Down and Airborne.

In this chapter, you'll learn how to set footstep timing the way you want it, and how to adjust it after it's been set. We'll also look at some common errors in footstep timing and how to correct them.

Displaying Footstep Keys

In the Track View - Dope Sheet window, you can edit the footstep keys in a number of ways to change the timing between one footstep to another.

To see the footstep keys, turn on Footstep mode in the Motion panel. Then open the Dope Sheet either by right-clicking in the viewport and choosing Dope Sheet, or by choosing Track View - Dope Sheet from the Graph Editors menu.

If Edit Ranges is your default mode for Dope Sheet, you'll have to change to Edit Keys mode. On the Dope Sheet toolbar, click Edit Keys, and then you'll be able to see the footstep keys in the Dope Sheet. You may not have to do this, if your installation is set to default to Edit Keys.

To see the individual biped keys, expand the Dope Sheet's Objects hierarchy in the left panel. Expand the Bip01 object, and find the Bip01 Footsteps level. The Transform track below that contains the footstep keys, represented by blue- and green-shaded boxes corresponding to the icon colors. Bright-colored boxes are inactive footsteps; pale boxes are the active footsteps.

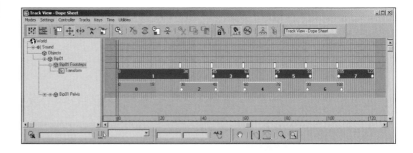

Each footstep box shows three *footstep key numbers*. The large, boldface number in the lower-center of the box is the footstep number. The number at the top-left shows the frame at which the footstep starts, and the number at the upper-right is the frame where it ends. (If the boxes are small, you may see only two numbers.)

The biped foot touches the ground at the first footstep frame and leaves the ground at the last frame. Even though the biped's foot might bend during that time, the foot is considered to be "in the footstep" from the first frame to the last frame, inclusive. When there is no footstep for a foot, it's in the air.

EXERCISE 5.1

Looking at Footstep Keys

This is a quick exercise to help you understand how footstep keys are represented in the Dope Sheet, and their relationship to biped motion.

1. Load the file `mybipedwalk.max` that you created in Chapter 4, or load `Walk.max` from the CD that comes with this book.

2. Select a biped body part and go to the Motion panel, and click ▦ Footstep Mode to turn it on.

3. Select the Bip01 object in the viewport, right-click and pick Dope Sheet to open the Track View - Dope Sheet window.

4. On the Dope Sheet toolbar, click ▦ Edit Keys if it's not already highlighted.

5. In the Dope Sheet left panel, scroll down to the Objects entries. Under Bip01, locate Bip01 Footsteps, and then the Transform track. If you don't see the footsteps in the key window, expand the hierarchy and select Transform.

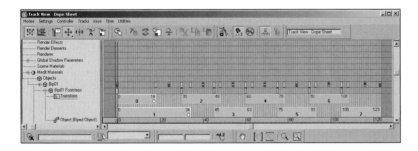

6. Play the animation, and observe the relationship between the footstep keys and the motion.

Notice that the keys alternate left and right, but overlap so that the biped is never completely airborne.

7. Load the file Run.max from the CD. Select any part of the biped, go to the Motion panel, and turn on Footstep mode. As you did before, open the Dope Sheet and expand the Bip01 Footsteps entry.

Again, notice the relationship between the motion and the footstep keys. The keys still alternate, but they no longer overlap; and where there are no footstep keys, the biped is in the air.

8. Load the file Jump.max from the CD. Perform the same procedure for displaying the footstep keys in the Dope Sheet.

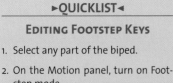

Notice the relationship between motion and footstep keys. This time, the footsteps don't alternate, so the biped keeps its feet together throughout the animation.

Changing Footstep Timing

By editing the footstep keys in the Dope Sheet, you can change footstep timing.

Before you edit footstep keys, it's a good practice to first deactivate the footsteps and then reactivate them after you've made all the desired changes. You'll see several benefits to this practice as we work through this chapter. To deactivate footsteps, you select them and then click ⬛ Deactivate Footsteps in the Footstep Operations rollout.

During the process of changing footstep placement or timing, some of your changes might cause problems that Character Studio feels it can't solve immediately. For example, if two footsteps

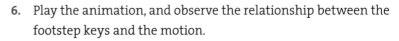

►QUICKLIST◄

EDITING FOOTSTEP KEYS

1. Select any part of the biped.

2. On the Motion panel, turn on Footstep mode.

3. Open the Dope Sheet.

4. Turn on Edit Keys.

5. Expand the hierarchy under Bip01 Footsteps.

6. Deactivate footsteps.

7. Move or resize keys as necessary.

8. Activate footsteps.

are too close together in time, the biped won't have time to lift its foot in between steps. You might be in the process of changing the timing to fix this problem, but Character Studio won't let you make the first change if footsteps are activated. You can solve this problem by deactivating footsteps before changing them.

There are three ways you can edit footstep keys:

- Change the start and/or end frame of the footstep key.

- Change the footstep key's placement on the time track, causing the entire footstep to occur at a different time.

- Delete the footstep key.

To change the frame at which a footstep starts or ends, click at the end of the footstep box until a small dot appears in the box. Click and drag the end of the box left to an earlier frame, or right to a later frame. The frame numbers in the box change accordingly, and the footstep key is enlarged or reduced. If you make a footstep key shorter, the foot will be in the footstep for a shorter period of time; if you enlarge it, the foot will stay in the step longer.

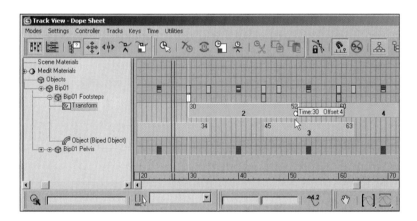

To move a footstep in time without changing its length, click the footstep to select it. A dot appears on each end of the footstep key. Drag the key to the left or right to its new time.

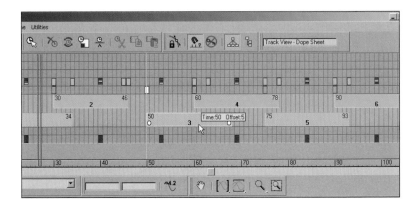

You can also move more than one footstep key at a time. Just select them all with one of the usual 3ds Max methods (Ctrl-clicking, or drawing a selection region around them). Then click and drag any of the selected footsteps to move them all at once.

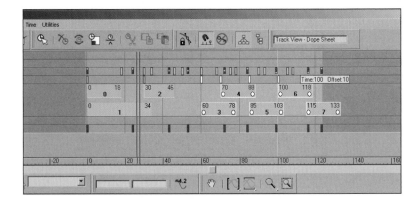

To delete one or more footstep keys, select the key in the usual way and click ⊠ Delete Footsteps on the Motion panel. This also deletes the footstep icon on the screen. When a footstep is deleted, the remaining footsteps automatically renumber themselves. Notice that only active footsteps can be deleted.

You can't always manipulate footstep keys in the Dope Sheet the way you'd like. Sometimes when you try to move a key, you'll get an error message telling you that what you want to do is not possible. For example, Character Studio won't allow you to overlap two footsteps for the same foot in the Dope Sheet. This makes sense—the biped's foot cannot be in two places at once. Character Studio also won't allow you to move footsteps into frames before frame 0.

Some operations are prohibited only when footsteps are active. One example would be trying to move a footstep very close in time to another footstep for the same foot. On the other hand, this operation is perfectly fine to do when footsteps are inactive. This is another reason to deactivate footsteps before making changes, and then reactivate them when you're done.

It's vital that you get footsteps' timing right *before* animating the upper body. This is because 3ds Max creates keys for a number of other body parts (hips, spine, and arms) when footstep keys are made. Every time you re-create keys for the footsteps, the default keys for the footsteps and the upper body parts are reset. This wipes out any changes you've made to the upper body keys, and you have to do them all over again. So be sure you get the footstep placement and timing as exact as possible before animating the upper body.

Time Between Footsteps

As you may remember from Chapter 1, footstep animation makes the biped react realistically to gravity. This is good if you're using realistic timing, bad if you're not.

In footstep animation, when the biped is in the air between footsteps, Character Studio calculates how high the biped would have to jump to stay in the air for that period. If it's in the air for 80 frames or more, the biped is going to take a giant leap into the stratosphere. Bipeds have infinitely strong legs, and they will leap as high as necessary to stay in the air during airborne periods.

A useful exercise is to have a friend jump up into the air while you time the jump. You don't need a stopwatch—just use the method of counting "one-1000, two-1000" to see how many seconds your friend can stay in the air. Chances are, your friend will come back to earth long before you say "three-1000."

Animation generally plays back at 15, 25, or 30 frames per second (the default frame rate in 3ds Max). Suppose you're creating an animation to play back at 30 frames per second: Those two seconds your friend is in the air translate into 60 frames.

EXERCISE 5.2

Leapin' Biped

This exercise illustrates what can happen when you give Character Studio too much time for a simple leap.

Deactivate Footsteps

1. Load the file JUMP.MAX from the CD that comes with this book.

    This file contains a sequence of eight jump footsteps, with three airborne periods between footsteps.

2. Select any part of the biped. On the Motion panel, click the Footstep Mode button.

3. Right-click in the viewport and choose Dope Sheet.

4. In the Dope Sheet window, navigate to the Bip01 > Bip01 Footsteps > Transform track in the hierarchy panel on the left to view the footsteps.

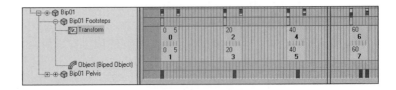

5. Select all the footsteps by dragging a region around them, in either a viewport or the Dope Sheet.

6. In the Footstep Operations rollout, click ⊞ Deactivate Footsteps.

▶TIP◀

Selecting footstep keys also selects footstep icons, and vice versa. So you can make your selection either in the Dope Sheet or in a viewport.

Increase the Gap Between Footsteps

1. In the Dope Sheet, select footstep keys 4 through 7. You can do this by dragging a region around them, or by holding down Ctrl as you click each key.

2. Click and drag the selected footstep keys to the end of the animation.

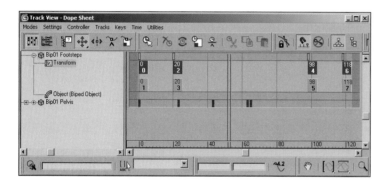

You can probably see what's coming next. What will the biped do between footsteps 2/3 and 4/5?

3. Close the Dope Sheet, or resize it so that you can easily see the biped in the Left or Perspective viewport.

4. In the Footstep Operations rollout, click ⊞ Create Keys for Inactive Footsteps.

5. Play the animation.

    Leapin' lizards! The biped goes right off screen between footsteps 2/3 and 4/5. It has nearly three seconds to jump, and jump it does!

You might think you could keep the biped from jumping so high by moving the COM downward during the airborne period, but

> **►NOTE◄**
>
> It is possible to make the biped refrain from jumping so high during long airborne periods without adjusting footstep timing. This is accomplished with freeform animation, which is covered in Chapter 7.

this won't work. Gravity is in charge here, so the COM will pop right back to its stratospheric position.

The way to fix an animation like this is to deactivate footsteps, then move the footsteps closer together in Track View before again creating keys for footsteps. The preceding exercise is here simply to show you this phenomenon, so if it happens to you, you'll know what's going on and how to fix it.

EXERCISE 5.3

Adjusting Footstep Timing

In this exercise, you'll adjust footstep timing to make an animation work better. First you'll increase the overall time of the animation, and then you'll adjust footstep keys, both as a group and individually.

View the Scene

1. Load the file `Splits.max` from the CD.

2. Play the animation.

   This file contains a biped taking a big step between footsteps 3 and 4. The biped doesn't have enough time to get to the next footstep without doing the splits, which is rather hard on the biped.

Deactivate Footsteps

1. Select any part of the biped, and click 👣 Footstep Mode in the Motion panel. Then select all the footsteps and click 👣 Deactivate Footsteps.

2. Right-click in the viewport and choose Dope Sheet.

3. In the Dope Sheet window object hierarchy, navigate to the Bipo1 > Bipo1 Footsteps > Transform track. Notice that the footstep keys are brightly colored because the footsteps are inactive.

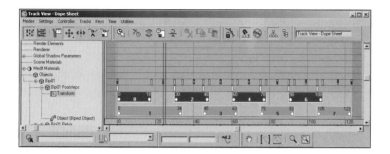

In order to make this animation work, what we need is more time between footsteps 3 and 4, which will cause footsteps 4 through 7 to occur later than they currently do. This would push some of the footsteps off the end of the active time segment. We'll need to have more frames in the animation.

4. Click ⊞ Time Configuration at the bottom-right of the screen. Change the Length parameter to 140.

Now you have room to put more time between footsteps 3 and 4. This will allow the biped to spend a little time hopping between these two footsteps.

5. In the Dope Sheet, click the [ ] Zoom Horizontal Extents button to see the entire length of the animation in the window, including the new frames at the end.

6. Select footstep keys 4 through 7, either by Ctrl-clicking or by drawing a selection region.

7. In the Dope Sheet, click and drag the selected footsteps to the right until the right end of footstep 7 is at the end of the animation.

This creates a gap between footsteps 3 and 4, which gives the biped time to be airborne.

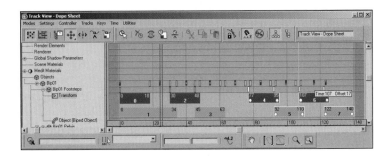

8. Click  Create Keys for Inactive Footsteps to reactivate the footsteps.

9. Play the animation.

Now that the biped has more time between footsteps 3 and 4, it makes a small jump between the two footsteps instead of contorting itself.

10. To make the jump look more natural, you can also move the footsteps in the viewport so that footsteps 4 through 7 are located closer to footstep 3 than before, which will close the gap that needs to be leapt.

11. Save the scene with the filename Leap.max.

EXERCISE 5.4

Dancing Gymnast

In this exercise, you'll put together everything you've learned so far to create a unique dance for the gymnast.

1. Load the file gymnast_no_anim.max from the CD that comes with this book.

   Let's create some new footsteps for the gymnast.

2. Select any part of the biped. On the Motion panel, click Footstep Mode.

3. In the Footstep Creation rollout, make sure the Walk gait is selected, and click Create Multiple Footsteps. In the Create Multiple Footsteps dialog, set Number of Footsteps to 8, then click OK to exit the dialog.

4. In the viewport, move the footsteps close to the biped. You will have to move each footstep individually.

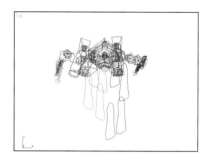

You've already seen this type of footstep sequence, in Chapter 4. The footsteps were created with a Walk gait, so the gymnast will shuffle from one footstep to another. But with what you now know about footstep timing, you can adjust the timing to make the animation more interesting.

5. Right-click in the viewport and choose Dope Sheet.

6. In the Dope Sheet, open the Bip01 object hierarchy to display the footsteps.

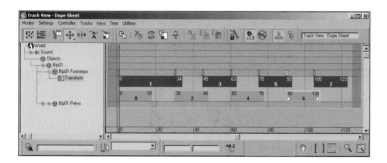

7. Click at the leftmost end of footstep key 5.

A dot appears at the leftmost end of the footstep key.

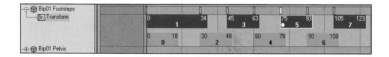

8. Drag the left end of footstep key 5 to the right until it is positioned to the right of footstep 4.

This shortens footstep 5 so that it starts later.

9. Click at the rightmost end of footstep key 4 to make the dot appear.

10. Drag the right end of footstep key 4 to the left until it's about the same length as footstep key 5.

    This creates a small hop between footsteps 4 and 5.

11. Close the Track View - Dope Sheet window.

12. Click ⬚ Create Keys for Inactive Footsteps, and play the animation.

    The gymnast steps from footstep to footstep and then does a short hop between footsteps 4 and 5.

    Feel free to continue editing the footstep timing for this little dance. Be sure to deactivate the footsteps and create new keys from time to time, to smooth out the animation. When Character Studio creates keys for the biped, it makes decisions about how much the ankles and knees will bend based on the distance and timing between footsteps. If you change the timing or placement of the footsteps substantially, the biped could bend its knees or ankles unnaturally.

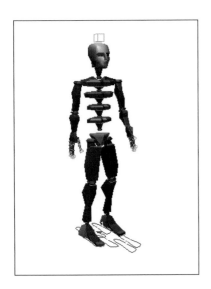

If you like, you can unhide the mesh to see how the animation is shaping up.

13. When you've finished working on the animation, save the file as gymnast_hopdance.max.

Animating Feet and Legs

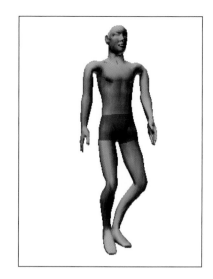

When a foot is *not* in a footstep, the foot and leg can be animated into another position by turning on the Auto Key button, or by using Biped's Set Key.

When a foot *is* in a footstep, you can't pull it out of the footstep. You can, however, rotate the foot so that just the heel or toes are touching the ground.

If you want to change the bend of the biped's knees in a footstep, click the Body Vertical button and move the COM up or down.

EXERCISE 5.5

Animating Legs and Feet

In this exercise, you'll adjust the biped's legs and feet.

1. Load the file Bump.max that you created in Chapter 4, or load it from the CD.

2. Move to frame 60 where the biped is stepping over the highest part of the bump.

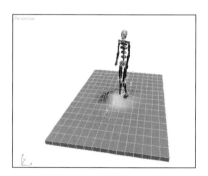

   In this animation, the biped's foot passes through the bump between frames 50 and 60. You're going to change the positions of the legs to make the biped step over the bump.

3. Turn on the ⏭ Key Mode Toggle. This will allow you to move from key to key more easily.

4. Select the foot that steps through the bump. This displays the leg keys on the trackbar at the bottom of the screen.

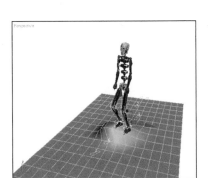

5. Use ▶| Next Key and |◀ Previous Key to move through the keyframes. Find the keyframes where the leg passes through the bump. (The Next Key and Previous Key buttons are active only when Key Mode Toggle is turned on.)

6. When you have found a key where the leg or foot passes through the bump, turn on the Auto Key button.

7. Move the biped's foot so that the knee bends more, and the foot passes over rather than through the bump.

   Because the leg isn't in a footstep, you can move it anywhere you like.

8. Locate any other keys where the leg passes through the bump. Move and rotate the foot as necessary to clear the bump as the leg passes over it.

9. Play the animation.

   The biped now steps over the bump at its highest point.

10. Save your animation as Bump_good.max.

Additional Exercises

Once you have the hang of creating footsteps and moving them around, try these additional exercises to learn more about working with Character Studio.

> **►NOTE◄**
>
> When you're working with regular animation keys and not footsteps, there's no need to deactivate footsteps. Deactivating footsteps is only necessary when the actual footsteps have been moved around.

EXERCISE 5.6

Backflip

In this exercise, you'll make the biped do a backflip.

1. Load the file ArmsUp.max from the CD, and play the animation.

   This scene contains a jumping biped.

2. Select any biped part. On the Motion panel, click the ⟳ Body Rotation button.

   This selects the COM and displays the COM rotation keys on the trackbar.

3. Turn on the 🔒 Selection Lock Toggle.

   This ensures that you will rotate the COM and not some other object by mistake.

4. Turn on the ⏮ Key Mode Toggle, and use ⏭ Next Key to go from one keyframe to the next.

   Notice that there are no rotation keys during the time the biped is jumping.

5. Move the time slider until the biped is about a third of the way through the second jump.

6. Turn on Auto Key.

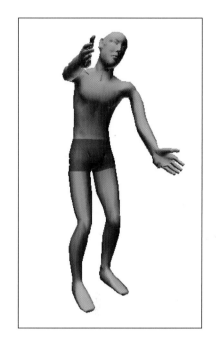

7. Rotate the COM on its local Y axis to make the biped's head point to a seven or eight o'clock position.

8. Move the time slider so that the biped is about two-thirds of the way through its jump.

   The biped's rotation will change during this time. This is normal, because the biped is moving into the next keys, where the footsteps are. Ignore this change and continue.

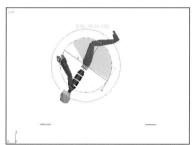

9. Rotate the COM on its Y axis to make the biped's head face the four o'clock position.

10. Play the animation.

    The biped does a quick flip in the air.

11. Here are a few other things to try: If you want the biped to jump higher, you can use the Dope Sheet to give it more time to jump. You can also animate the arms and legs to a curl position during the flip, to make it look more realistic. You can rotate the feet, as well, to complete the effect.

12. Save your animation as `ArmsUp_backflip.max`.

Hopscotch

In this exercise, you'll make a biped play hopscotch.

1. Load the file Hopscotch.max from the CD.

   This file contains a hopscotch grid. The grid is upside down when viewed in the Top viewport. When the biped is created, it will be facing the correct direction to hop through the squares.

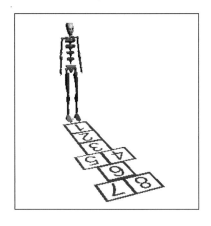

2. Create a biped about 200 units high near hopscotch square 1.

3. On the Motion panel, turn on Footstep mode. In the Footstep Creation rollout, choose the 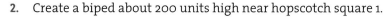 Jump gait and click Create Multiple Footsteps.

4. In the Create Multiple Footsteps dialog, set the Actual Stride Length to 50. Set the Number of Footsteps to 14. Click OK to create the footsteps.

   The Actual Stride Length value relates to the approximate distance between each square. Setting this distance will make the footsteps fall into the correct general area.

5. In the viewport, move the footsteps onto the hopscotch squares.

6. In the viewport, select and delete any unnecessary footsteps. For example, if the biped is to hop on its right foot on squares 1 through 3, then you don't need the first three left footsteps.

7. Click ⊡ Create Keys for Inactive Footsteps, and play the animation.

The biped hops from square to square. (Of course, you would want to animate the head, arms, and spine to make the biped jump more realistically.)

8. Save your file as Hopscotch_Anim.max.

Now you have the basics of editing footsteps. Doing this with confidence takes practice, so go ahead and choreograph your own movements for the biped. Work with footstep placement and timing until the biped does what you want it to do.

> ►TIP◄
>
> When editing footsteps, get in the habit of looking at the biped from the waist down until its leg movements are right; then go on to working with the upper body.

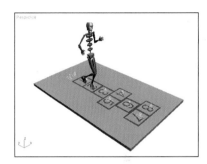

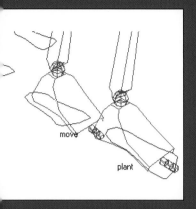

CHAPTER 6

Advanced Footsteps

As you're probably beginning to see, there are many ways to work with footsteps—all designed to create the animation you want with a minimum of effort. By working with footstep placement and numbering, and with the footstep keys in the Dope Sheet, you can make almost anything happen with footsteps.

In this chapter, you'll move on from automatic footsteps to manual placement. Automatic footsteps can provide you with a basis for your animation, but manual placement and timing is necessary for most custom sequences.

Manual Footstep Placement

For working out a footstep sequence, the best tools are your own feet and a pencil and paper. Any expert character animator will assure you that all good character animators, without exception, get up and act out a sequence before ever starting to animate it. The value of this practice cannot be emphasized strongly enough— if you don't get up and act it out, you won't be able to animate it effectively. A strong, smooth animation is produced when you act it out; when you don't, you get boring, stilted, unconvincing animation. You might feel silly when you get up and act out a dance, but you won't feel so silly when your animation turns out better than you ever thought possible.

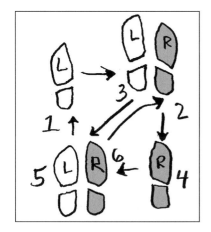

After you've physically practiced the movement you want, spend a little time with pencil and paper working out the placement, number, and side (left/right) for each footstep. Then when you go to place them in Character Studio, you can concentrate on the methods used rather than where the footsteps go. Even experienced animators find their work easier if they draw the footstep placement first before actually placing them.

You've already learned how to create footsteps automatically with the [icon] Create Multiple Footsteps button. Now you'll see how to place footsteps individually, exactly where you want them.

If you already have some footsteps in your scene, the [icon] Create Footsteps (Append) button becomes available on the Footstep Creation rollout. To place footsteps manually, you click this button and then move the cursor over a viewport. The cursor shows you whether a left or right footstep is about to be placed. Simply click in the scene to place the footstep. Click again to place a footstep for the opposite foot, or press Alt+Q on the keyboard to toggle between a left and right footstep. The new footsteps will be numbered in sequence starting after the last existing footstep.

The 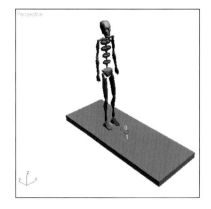 Create Footsteps (At Current Frame) button can also be used to place footsteps. However, you must take a lot of care when using this option. If a footstep for a particular foot already exists at the current frame, you will not be able to place a footstep. If footsteps exist after the current frame, the footstep placed at the current frame will receive a number appropriate for its place in the chronology, thus shifting footstep numbers (possibly a lot of them) after it. This can cause problems if you're working with notes that refer to specific footstep numbers.

In general, you should use Create Footsteps (At Current Frame) to place the first footstep when no footsteps exist, and then use Create Footsteps (Append) to manually place the rest of the footsteps.

Often, the best solution for creating footsteps is a combination of the automatic and manual methods. For example, suppose you have a character that does a little swing dance step, then walks up to another character and asks her to dance. The first part—the dance step—would be easier to create with manual footsteps, but the walk that follows could be made with an automatic walk sequence.

EXERCISE 6.1

Footstep Placement Practice

In this exercise, you'll choreograph a very simple dance and then work out the footstep placement for it using just pencil, paper, and your own two feet.

1. Get out of your chair and stand up. Choreograph a simple, short dance of your own making, with eight or fewer steps, and perform the steps yourself.

2. Repeat the dance a few times until you're sure of how it goes.

3. Get a pencil (best for erasing as needed) and some paper with no lines.

4. On the paper, draw the dance footsteps in sequence. On each footstep, write the footstep number, with *L* for left or *R* for right.

   Remember that the biped always starts out by standing on footsteps 0 and 1.

5. Reset 3ds Max. Create a biped of any size.

6. On the Motion Panel, turn on Footstep Mode. Click the Create Footsteps (At Current Frame) button. In a viewport, click to place footsteps 0 and 1 to indicate where the biped will stand at the start of the dance.

7. Continue placing the steps for your dance. Press Alt+Q to toggle between left and right steps (for example, when you've choreographed two left steps in a row).

8. Move, rotate, and delete footsteps as necessary to get the arrangement on the screen to look like the one you have drawn on paper.

   Don't try to create keys for the footsteps at this point. The animation probably won't be right because you haven't worked with the timing yet. The purpose of this exercise is just to give you experience placing footsteps and getting them right.

9. Save the file as DANCE01.MAX.

▶TIP◀

There may be times when you want one foot to step twice in a row, as in a dance. When you place footsteps, they always alternate feet, but you can manually switch feet with Alt+Q. Another way to get this to happen is to delete the intermediate left footstep, as in the Chapter 5 "Hopscotch" exercise. The remaining footsteps will renumber themselves accordingly.

Advanced Footstep Timing

In Chapter 4, you learned how to create footsteps automatically. In Chapter 5, you looked at the timing in Track View - Dope Sheet and made a few modifications to the timing to see how it would affect the animation.

When you create auto footsteps, Character Studio automatically sets the timing for the footsteps according to the gait chosen and various values such as Walk Footstep and Double Support that you can change on the Create Multiple Footsteps dialog. When placing footsteps manually, you change these values on the Footstep Creation rollout before you place the footsteps, and you'll usually have to make extensive adjustments to footstep timing in the Dope Sheet.

Timing Parameters

Gait	No Feet on Ground	One Foot on Ground	Both Feet on Ground
Walk	N/A	Walk Footstep	Double Support
Run	Airborne	Run Footstep	N/A
Jump	Airborne	N/A	2 Feet Down

Footstep Key Parts

Keys in 3ds Max are usually set on a specific frame. Footstep keys, on the other hand, can last several frames. There are four parts to every footstep key, one for each part of the foot's motion. These are called *leg states*.

- *Touch:* When the foot touches down. This key is one frame long, just before a Plant.

- *Plant:* Between Touch and Lift, when the foot is flat. This key is usually several frames long.

- *Lift:* Then the foot lifts off. This key is one frame long, just after a Plant.

- *Move:* When the foot is in the air and not in a footstep at all. This key is usually several frames long.

You can see the leg state by turning on ⬛ Leg States in the Biped rollout; then choose Modes and Display > Display Group. The leg state's label shows in the viewport next to the footstep.

There's no great secret to setting up footsteps accurately and quickly. It's just a matter of practice. This next exercise will provide you with some practice in footstep timing techniques. After that, your best bet is to think up new movement patterns and see how accurately you can represent them in footsteps on your own.

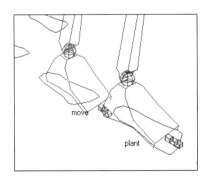

EXERCISE 6.2

Footstep Timing

When working out the timing for footsteps, you'll find it very helpful to make a rough sketch of how the footstep keys should look in the Dope Sheet. Also, count out the total length of time; it then becomes a simple matter to adjust the Dope Sheet to match your plan.

1. Work out how the Dope Sheet should look for a simple two-step dance, and draw on paper the general appearance of the footstep keys.

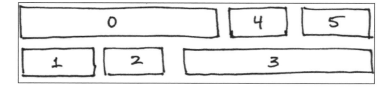

2. Reset 3ds Max, and create a biped. Then create a six-step sequence of your dance, using any footstep method.

3. Open the Dope Sheet and display the footsteps. Compare the footsteps to your sketch, and see what adjustments are necessary to make them match.

4. Work out how the Dope Sheet should look for each of the following sequences. For each sequence, draw on paper the general appearance of the footstep keys in the Dope Sheet. The correct drawings appear at the end of this exercise. Check your work against these drawings.

    - Both feet staying down the whole time

    - Walking in circles, then staying still

    - One foot staying still while the other moves back and forth

    - One foot staying still while the other moves back and forth; then that moving foot is placed down and stays still while the other moves around

Your Dance Timing

1. Work out the Dope Sheet pattern for the dance you choreo-graphed in the preceding exercise, and draw it on a piece of paper.

2. Load the file DANCE01.MAX that you saved earlier.

3. Open the Dope Sheet and display the footsteps tracks.

4. Adjust the Dope Sheet timing so that it looks like your drawing.

   You can move an entire footstep by dragging it from its center. You can also lengthen or shorten a footstep by dragging one end of it.

5. Click [icon] Create Keys for Inactive Footsteps.

6. Watch the animation.

   Does the biped's motion roughly match your choreography? If so, congratulations! If not, see if you can figure out where it went wrong. Deactivate the footsteps, change the footstep timing, and create keys for the footsteps again.

7. Save the file as DANCE02.MAX.

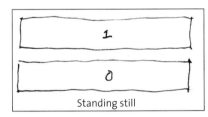

Standing still

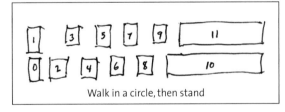

Walk in a circle, then stand

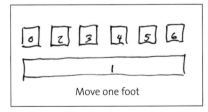

Move one foot

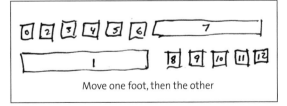

Move one foot, then the other

Accelerating Gravity

You'll recall from the "Leapin' Biped" exercise in Chapter 5 that Character Studio automatically figures out the biped's reactions to natural laws such as gravity. You can, however, adjust the height of a jump when a biped is entirely airborne (in a run or jump, for example). You do this by changing the GravAccel parameter on the Dynamics & Adaptation rollout.

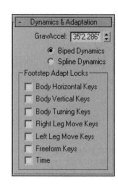

The default GravAccel value is based on the biped's height and determines the strength of gravity in the scene. This in turn determines how high the biped jumps. In Character Studio, gravity is always calculated based on the idea that the biped is 5' 10" tall (the average height for a human being), and that gravity is about 10 m/sec^2 (the strength of gravity on Earth). For characters that are very tall, short, light, or heavy, or for environments where gravity should be stronger or weaker than Earth's, the default GravAccel calculation might not produce the results you want.

You can also change the value of GravAccel to create cartoonish effects, such as characters jumping or bouncing very high. When GravAccel is reduced, the biped doesn't jump as high; when it is increased, the biped jumps higher.

The GravAccel value is the same throughout the animation, and cannot be animated. After you've changed the GravAccel parameter, there is no way to return to the default value automatically. It's a good idea to write down the original GravAccel value before changing it, so you can always return to it later if need be.

EXERCISE 6.3
Changing Jump Height

In this exercise, you'll adjust the GravAccel parameter to change the height of the biped's jump.

1. Load the file JUMP.MAX from the Chapter 5 folder on the CD, and play the animation.

The biped jumps three times over the course of the animation.

2. Move the time slider to an area of the animation where the biped is airborne.

3. Expand the Dynamics & Adaptation rollout.

4. Write the GravAccel value down on a piece of paper.

   The GravAccel value is calculated based on the biped's height. Notice that the value for this biped is 733.559. For your own bipeds, it will be different.

5. Increase GravAccel to approximately three times its current value, to 2200.

6. Play the animation.

   The biped now jumps higher throughout the entire animation.

7. Decrease the GravAccel parameter to about half its original value, about 365. Play the animation.

   The biped's jumps now have less height throughout the animation.

Balance Factor

When you create keys for footsteps, Character Studio automatically figures out your biped's *balance point*. But as with other parameters, this basic result can look a little stiff, so you adjust the biped's balance using the Balance Factor. This option is available only when you use footsteps to animate the biped (as opposed to freeform animation).

To see how Balance Factor works, let's take a look at how your own body reacts when you're standing on two feet. When you're standing up and you bend forward, your hips shift backward to compensate for the additional weight in front of your body. The biped works in the same way. When you rotate the biped's spine forward, backward, or side-to-side, the biped's hips shift in the opposite direction.

There may be times when you want the hips to move less or to stay still, or you'll want them to move more than the default amount. The Balance Factor parameter can be used to adjust the biped in this way.

The Balance Factor can range from 0 to 2. The default of 1 puts the biped's weight between the COM and the head. When Balance Factor is 0, the weight is at the COM, which keeps the COM still while the upper body moves. With Balance Factor at 2, the weight is in the head, which keeps the head steady while the hips move.

The Balance Factor parameter is located near the bottom of the Key Info rollout. Expand the Body section to display the Balance Factor field.

The Balance Factor can be animated to cause the biped to react differently and shift its weight during different parts of the animation.

EXERCISE 6.4

Standing Up

In this exercise, you'll animate the Balance Factor to make a biped get up out of its chair.

1. Load the file Sitting.max from the CD.

   This file contains a biped sitting on a chair. The biped has two footsteps under its feet for 100 frames, but no other animation.

   First, we want to animate the biped bending over to swing itself out of the chair.

2. Turn on Auto Key.

3. Go to frame 10.

4. Select the lowest spine link, Bip01 Spine.

5. In the Left viewport, rotate the spine link forward by about 60 degrees.

   The biped's hips shift backward in the chair. Not very realistic!

6. Press Ctrl+Z to undo the spine link rotation.

Keep the Hips Still

To make the hips stay still as the spine rotates forward, we'll change the Balance Factor.

1. Go to frame 0.

2. Click ↔ Body Horizontal.

   Remember, the Balance Factor parameter can be changed only when Body Horizontal is selected and a Body Horizontal key exists at the current frame.

3. Locate the Balance Factor parameter at the bottom of the Key Info rollout, in the Body section. Expand the Body section if necessary.

   Because there is already a Body Horizontal key on frame 0, the Balance Factor parameter is available.

4. Change the Balance Factor to 0.

   This shifts the biped's balance all the way to COM.

5. Go to frame 10.

6. Click ⊙ Set Key to set a Body Horizontal key.

   This sets the Balance Factor to 0 at frame 10, which will keep the hips still from frames 0 through 10 as the biped bends over in the chair.

7. Select the lowest spine link, and rotate it forward again by about 60 degrees.

   This time, the biped's hips stay still as it bends forward.

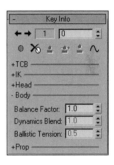

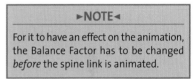

Swing the Weight Forward

To give the biped enough leverage to get up out of the chair, we want its arms to swing forward and its weight to move forward to its head. This will be simulated by changing the Balance Factor to 2.

1. Still on frame 10, rotate the arms forward and the head downward to show the position of a person rising from a chair.

2. Click ⬍ Body Vertical, and click ⊙ Set Key.

   This sets a Body Vertical key in the current position. The biped will be getting up in a moment, and we want it to stay sitting up until frame 10.

3. Go to frame 20.

4. Click ↔ Body Horizontal, and click ⊙ Set Key.

   The hips stay still from 0 to 20, while the arms and head move from 0 through 10.

5. Change the Balance Factor to 2.

   The COM moves forward to a position somewhere near the biped's knees, indicating that its weight is being thrown forward.

6. Move the COM upward and forward so that the biped is in a squatting position, with its shoulders about halfway between its hips and its knees.

Balance for Standing

Now the biped is just about ready to raise its body up into a normal standing position, returning to the default Balance Factor of 1.

1. Go to frame 30.

2. Click ↔ Body Horizontal, and click ⊙ Set Key.

3. Change the Balance Factor to 1.

   The COM moves back toward the biped's body.

4. Rotate the lowest spine link so that the spine is once again straight.

5. Move the COM to bring the biped into a standing position.

6. Rotate the head to look forward, and rotate the arms to fall by the biped's sides.

7. Play the animation, and watch the biped get up out of its chair.

8. Save the file as `standing.max` in your folder.

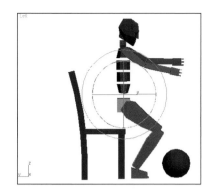

Converting to Freeform

Using footsteps is a workable means to lay out animation. However, footsteps follow particular rules and behaviors, which makes them less useful for custom animation.

To make your animation sequences fully customizable, you can convert your footstep animation into standard freeform animation with the simple click of the Convert button. Once you've converted the animation, you can edit it using all the techniques that 3ds Max provides. You can even convert the freeform version back to footsteps afterward, if you want (which we'll look at in Chapter 9).

To convert a footstep animation to freeform, select the biped for which footsteps have been created. Then click the [⟳] Convert button on the Biped rollout. The Convert to Freeform dialog appears.

When converting to freeform animation, you have the option to generate a keyframe per frame. Doing this ensures that all the animation you had in the footstep animation will be preserved in the freeform variation. However, having a keyframe on each frame can complicate editing. You can turn on this option, or leave it off and use the Workbench to reduce the number of keys (see Chapter 8 for more about the Workbench).

Click OK to complete the conversion.

Once you have converted the footsteps to freeform animation, the footsteps disappear from the scene. You can then animate the biped with freeform methods, which are described in Section Three.

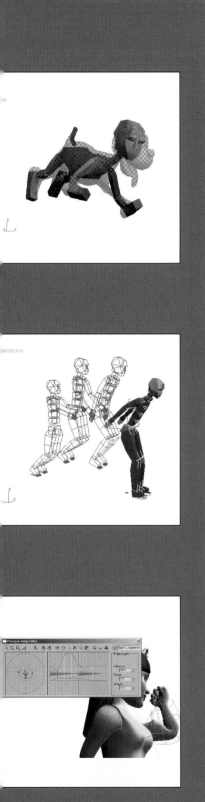

Freeform Animation

So far you've worked with footsteps, so Character Studio has taken care of a lot of the details for you. As you become more skilled with Character Studio, however, you'll want to animate your characters without footsteps, determining every detail, and making your own decisions. This method, called *freeform animation,* of course requires more knowledge of traditional animation principles. But in return, you get a lot more freedom when animating your character.

Freeform animation is useful when the biped's feet don't have to stick to the ground at any point, as when swimming or flying, for example. You can also use this type of animation to simulate footstep animation for an ordinary biped, or for unusual characters such as quadrupeds.

Most body animation is done in freeform mode, generating and moving keys as necessary. Freeform animation tools are also used to make a biped's hands or feet follow an object. It's much like the standard animation that you do in 3ds Max, but with fewer rules to follow and a simpler workflow.

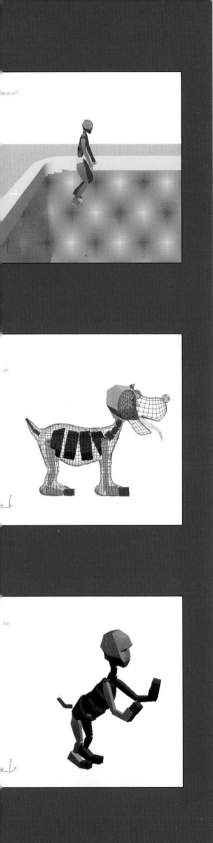

CHAPTER 7

Animating with Freeform

Freeform animation is the kind of animation you'll probably use most in your work. When your characters are swimming, sitting, speaking, doing yoga, and most other such activities, freeform animation, not footsteps, will be your mode of operation.

Freeform animation is really standard 3ds Max animation: You can set keys using Auto Key, moving or rotating body parts to create the transforms. You can also use Biped's specialized Set Key buttons, such as Set Planted Key to fix the foot or hand in space, or IK Blend to fix it to an object.

The main difference between freeform animation and standard 3ds Max animation is that with freeform you're using a Biped skeleton instead of a standard hierarchy of 3ds Max bones. The limitations of the Biped skeleton's movement match the limitations of a human skeleton's movement—at least, they try to. So why use Biped? Because it creates a linked and rigged skeleton in a split second. Biped has built-in FK/IK switching that you don't have to think about; it just works. And it lets you animate the pivots on hands and feet, which is very useful in everyday animation.

Using Freeform Mode

Creating a freeform animation is easy—just turn on the Auto Key button and start animating the biped, or select a biped body part and click ⊙ Set Key. After you've started a freeform animation, all the biped parts are still linked and can be animated, but the Footstep Mode button is grayed out, and all footstep operations are disabled. You are now working in *freeform mode*.

In the following exercise, you'll see that freeform animation takes a little more effort and knowledge of animation concepts. But it also allows you to construct a wider variety of animations than what you can do with footstep animation alone.

EXERCISE 7.1

Creating a Freeform Animation

In this exercise, you'll create a freeform animation of a biped sitting up in bed. Obviously, footsteps wouldn't be applicable for this type of animation, so freeform is the choice.

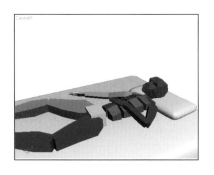

1. Load the file `Sleeping.max` from the CD. This file contains a biped sleeping peacefully on a bed.

2. Select the entire biped by going to the main toolbar, clicking the Named Selection Sets drop-down, and choosing `Biped`.

    In the first sitting motion, nearly every part of the biped's body will be animated. To keep the body in its current position at frame 0, you'll need to set keys for all body parts at frame 0.

3. Go to frame 0, and in the Key Info rollout of the Motion panel, click ⊙ Set Key.

Keys are set at frame 0 for all the selected biped parts. Now you're ready to start animating.

4. Click the Auto Key button to animate in Freeform mode.

5. Go to frame 20.

6. Select the lowest spine link, and rotate the biped's upper body into a sitting position.

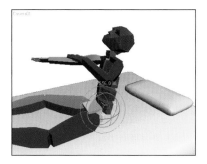

7. Position the remainder of the body to complete the sitting position, as shown.

8. Scrub through the animation by pulling the time slider.

Clean Up the Animation

Although frames 0 and 20 look fine, the biped's hands pass through the bed on the interim frames. So let's set additional keys between the two we've already set.

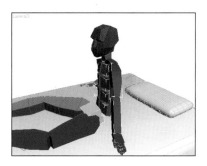

1. Make sure Auto Key is on.

2. Go to frame 5, and move the biped's left hand upward and away from the body.

   Also, position the right hand on the surface of the bed. Use the Move and Rotate tools to get the hand into the correct pose.

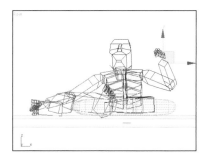

3. On frame 10, position both hands flat on the bed.

4. Move to frame 15, and again position the hands flat on the bed.

5. Play the animation.

   It's pretty convincing—as long as you don't look at the biped below the waist!

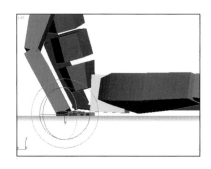

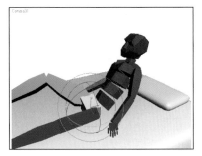

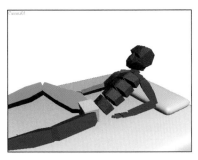

> **▶NOTE◄**
>
> Remember that you *rotate* the parent with FK, or *move* the child with IK.

> **▶TIP◄**
>
> The creation of IK solvers and bone structures is called *character rigging*. It is a complex and complicated task: a full-time job for technical directors at animation studios. The beauty of Character Studio is that the inverse kinematics are set up automatically when you create a biped.

6. At frame 20, add animation to the feet and thighs:

   Move the feet closer to the pelvis, causing the knees to bend.

   Rotate the thighs upward and over so that the legs look realistic.

   You can rotate the pelvis, if you'd like, to complete the animation.

7. Save the file with the name Wakeup.max in your folder. You can also see a finished version of this scene in the file Wakeup.max on the CD.

Exploring Forward and Inverse Kinematics

You may remember from Chapter 1, "Character Studio Basics," that 3ds Max uses two types of animation with linked objects: *forward kinematics (FK)*, in which the child object follows the parent, and *inverse kinematics (IK)*, in which the parent object follows a child.

Ordinarily, 3ds Max uses FK by default. IK is enabled when you set up an IK chain by using Animation > IK Solvers, or when you use interactive IK on any hierarchy by using the IK button on the Hierarchy panel. But in animating the biped, in both footstep and freeform modes, Character Studio makes liberal use of IK, automatically switching between FK and IK based on what you're doing.

Character Studio swaps between FK and IK automatically depending on whether you're moving or rotating the *end effector* (the child object on the chain that, when moved, affects parent objects in the chain). In order for the automatic FK/IK swapping to work during the animation process, Character Studio imposes these limitations:

- IK is in effect only when a hand/arm or foot/leg is moved (not rotated).

- While IK is in effect, the animation is passed only so far up the chain. For example, if you move the biped's foot, the leg moves and rotates accordingly, but the COM and spine do not.

IK Blend and Body/Object Parameters

In addition to determining how the rest of the body reacts when the feet and hands are moved, Character Studio also provides IK tools that do the opposite: determining how the feet and hands react when the rest of the body is moved.

The IK Blend and Body/Object parameters in the Key Info rollout determine how the hands and feet will react when the COM is moved. Each hand and foot can have its own parameter settings.

- When IK Blend is 0 and Body is selected (the default settings), FK is in effect. This means any animation of the COM will cause the hands and feet to follow along with the body.

- When IK Blend is 1 and Object is selected, the hand or foot will stay put while the COM moves the body, and the arms and legs react accordingly.

One of the special features of Character Studio is the IK Key buttons in the Key Info rollout. These buttons, available only when a leg or arm is selected, automatically set the IK Blend and Body/Object parameters to frequently used settings. The two buttons you'll use most often are ▣ Set Planted Key, which sets IK Blend to 1 and selects Object, and ▣ Set Free Key, which sets IK Blend to 0 and selects Body.

Think of Set Planted Key as telling a hand or foot to stay put, no matter what. Set Free Key tells a hand or foot to move when the COM or spine is moved.

EXERCISE 7.2

Push-Ups

In this exercise, you'll animate a biped doing push-ups. To make the hands and feet stay still while the body moves up and down, you'll use Set Planted Key. But first, let's see what happens when

we move the COM downward without making any changes to the IK settings.

1. Load the file `Pushup_Pose.max` from the CD.

   This is a scene with a biped ready to do push-ups. There is no animation in the scene yet. Keys have been set for some of the body parts when the biped was posed at frame 0, so the animation is already in freeform mode.

2. Select any part of the biped, go to the Motion panel, and click ⬍ Body Vertical.

3. Turn on the Auto Key button.

4. In the Left viewport, move the COM downward.

   The entire biped moves downward. This isn't what we want!

5. Click ↶ Undo to undo the movement of the COM.

Set the IK Keys

Now we'll set the IK Blend and Body/Object parameters with IK key buttons to make the hands and feet stay still while the COM moves.

1. Select the biped's right hand.

2. Go to the Motion panel, and expand the Key Info rollout.

3. Click 👤 Set Planted Key.

   The IK Blend parameter is set to 1, and Object is selected.

4. Select the left hand, and click 👤 Set Planted Key.

5. Select one of the feet, and click 👤 Set Planted Key.

   Here, you're selecting the actual hands and feet—but in fact, because it's IK, you can select any part of the arm or leg to set a key for the hand or foot.

6. To quickly select the opposite foot, go to the Track Selection rollout and click ⬌ Opposite. Now again click 👤 Set Planted Key.

Now each hand and each foot has a planted key set for it, so they're all fixed in space. If we animate the COM now, the limbs and legs will have to rotate to compensate for the extremities being planted.

Animate the Push-Ups

Try again to move the COM downward.

1. Go to frame 20.

2. Click ⬍ Body Vertical.

3. Turn on Auto Key if it isn't already.

4. In the Left viewport, move the COM downward by two or three units until the biped's knees almost touch the ground.

   This time, the biped's hands and feet stay put while the arms bend according to the new COM position.

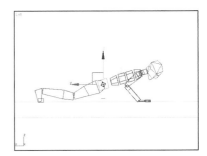

5. To improve the animation, you can add rotation keys to the lowest spine element so that the biped's chest also touches the ground at frame 20. Don't forget to add a rotation key at frame 0, as well, to make the biped straighten out its spine when the arms are extended.

6. Play the animation.

   The biped does a push-up!

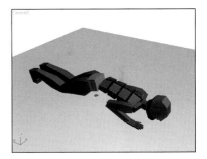

In Chapter 8, "Body Animation," you'll learn how to copy postures, so you can make the animation loop. A finished version of this scene can be found in the file `Pushup_Anim.max` on the CD.

Animating the IK Settings

The IK Blend and Body/Object settings can be animated to cause a hand or foot to stay still sometimes and move with the body at other times—which, as you'll recall from Chapter 1, is basically how a character walks: First a foot is stuck down to the floor while the remainder of the body moves. Then, when the other foot is planted on the floor, the foot moves along with the body.

Because the hands as well as the feet can be animated in this way, by animating IK Blend and Body/Object you can make a quadruped walk.

EXERCISE 7.3

Walking the Dog

In this exercise you'll use the IK key buttons to quickly and easily animate a quadruped—a dog—to make it walk. As you'll see, you set a planted key to make the foot or hand stay still, and set a free key to make it move. You can animate the pivoting action at the heel and off the toes, as well. First, however, we'll get the biped ready for its walk by setting keys and IK parameters at frame 0.

1. Load the file HappyDog.max from the CD.

   This file contains a happy little dog. A biped has already been set up for the mesh.

2. Unhide the named selection set Biped. When you see the message regarding hidden or frozen objects, answer Yes.

   The dog biped has already been associated with the mesh, and the Physique envelopes have been adjusted.

3. Select the named selection set Dog Parts, and hide these objects.

   The mesh and eyes have been hidden, leaving just the biped.

4. Select any part of the biped and go to the Motion panel.

5. Go to frame 0.

6. Click ↔ Body Horizontal, and then click ◉ Set Key.

7. Select the biped's right hand (the dog's right-front paw) and click 👤 Set Planted Key.

►NOTE◄

Remember that you can select any part of an arm or leg to set a key for the hand or foot.

8. Repeat step 7 for the left hand (left-front paw), and for each foot (the rear paws).

Now that all four paws are glued down, let's test the settings by putting the dog into a slight crouch to prepare for the walk.

9. Click ⬍ Body Vertical.

10. Turn on the Auto Key button.

11. Move the dog's COM downward by about 10 units. This sets a Body Vertical key.

12. Also, move the COM slightly backward to set a Body Horizontal key.

Take the First Step

Now we'll begin the walk cycle. We'll give the dog a cartoon-style walk: right leg and left arm moving at the same time, then left leg and right arm.

1. Go to frame 10.

   When a leg is moving through the air, it's following the body, which calls for an IK Blend of 0 and the Body option selected—so you can use Set Free Key.

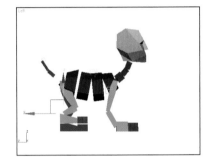

2. Select any part of the right leg and click ⬛ Set Free Key.

3. Select the left arm, and click ⬛ Set Free Key.

4. Make sure Auto Key is still on. In the Left viewport, move the right foot upward to a stepping position.

5. Select the left hand, and move it upward and slightly forward.

6. Move the COM upward until the dog's stationary legs are nearly straight.

7. Go to frame 20, and move the COM downward and forward.

   The lifted hand and foot will move with the COM while the others stay planted.

8. Move the lifted hand and foot forward and downward to be on the ground. You might have to rotate the hand to make it sit flat.

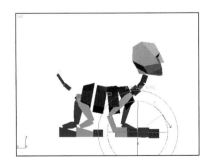

9. Set a planted key for the left hand and right foot that have just landed on the ground.

You have made the dog take one step. Now use the same process to make the dog take a second step.

Continue the Walk

Before going on, you need to set planted keys for the left foot and right hand, which have remained planted all this time but are about to move.

1. On frame 20, set a planted key for the right hand and left foot.

2. Go to frame 30.

3. Select the right hand and click ▣ Set Free Key. Then move the right hand upward and forward.

4. Select the left foot and click ▣ Set Free Key. Then move the left foot upward.

5. Move the COM forward and upward until the biped's weight is centered over its body, and the stationary arm is nearly straight.

6. Go to frame 40.

7. Move the COM downward and forward.

8. Place the right hand and left foot on the ground.

9. Set a planted key for the right hand and left foot.

10. Set a planted key for the left hand and right foot as well.

The basic walk cycle is complete. Do you see the pattern here? Set Planted Key is for when the leg or arm sticks to the ground, and Set Free Key is for when the arm or leg moves with the body.

11. Scrub through the animation to see how it looks.

12. Unhide the selection set Dog Parts, and hide the selection set Biped. Play the animation.

13. Save the file with the name `HappyDogWalk.max` in your folder.

You'll find a finished version of this exercise in the file `HappyDogWalk.max` on the CD.

Next, you'll work on making a walk look better with some additional freeform animation tools. (To find out how to make a looping walk cycle, see Chapter 10, "Motion Mixer and Motion Flow.")

More Freeform Tools

You may have noticed that when you click ▨ Set Planted Key, this also checks the Join to Prev IK Key checkbox in the IK section of the Key Info rollout. When Join to Prev IK Key is checked and the previous key's IK Blend value is set to 1 (as with a planted key), the foot or hand is forced to the same position it was in on the last key.

This feature is handy when you want a foot or hand to stay still at a frame where that foot or hand is already animated. When you click Set Planted Key and the previous key is a planted key, the foot or hand will snap to the same position as on the previous key.

Animating Pivot Points

In animating the dog walk, we placed the feet and hands flat on the ground with each step. Characters with toes, like our dog, usually step down heel first, and then rotate through the foot to bring up the heel while the toes stay on the ground.

By default, a biped has *animated pivot points* on the hands and feet that change as the biped moves through the walking motion. (Select a hand or foot and move from one key to the next; you'll see its current pivot point as a red dot.) In order to create a smoother walk, we'll need to change the default pivot points at certain points in the animation. In other words, we'll have to use animated pivot points.

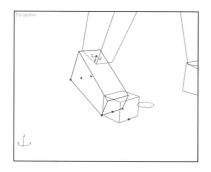

Selecting a new pivot point is simple: You click the Select Pivot button in the IK section of the Key Info rollout. (This button is available only when a leg, foot, arm, or hand is selected *and* a key exists for the biped part.) When Select Pivot is on, all possible locations for the new pivot point appear as blue dots on the biped part. Click to select the new pivot point; then click Select Pivot again to turn it off. The pivot is set for the current frame—you don't even have to turn on the Auto Key button when selecting pivots that can be animated.

EXERCISE 7.4

Doing an Articulated Walk

In this exercise, you'll use animated pivot points and other freeform features to refine the walking dog.

1. Load the file HappyDogWalk.max that you created earlier, or load the file from the CD.

2. Select the selection set Dog Parts, and hide the objects.

3. Unhide the selection set Biped.

4. Select any part of the biped, and go to the Motion panel.

5. Go to frame 20.

   This is the frame where the right foot and left hand step down. We want to make the right foot come down heel first, before placing the entire foot on the ground.

6. Turn on the Auto Key button.

7. Rotate the right foot.

   The foot currently rotates from the ball of the foot; however, we want the foot to rotate from the heel.

8. Undo any rotation you have just set.

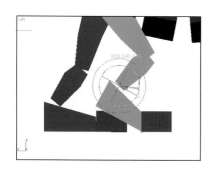

Change the Pivot Point

1. With the right foot still selected, expand the IK section on the Key Info rollout, and click Select Pivot.

►TIP◄

If you can't see the pivot points, change the viewport to Wireframe. Change the viewport back to Smooth and Highlights when you're done.

2. Click one of the pivot points at the heel of the right foot to turn it red.

3. Click Select Pivot to turn it off.

4. Rotate the right foot upward.

   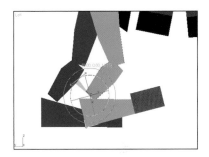

   The foot rotates from the heel, just as we'd like it to. And we've animated the pivot point from its location at the ball of the foot at frame 0, to the heel at frame 20.

5. Go to frame 25, and rotate the foot to make it sit flat on the ground.

   You can repeat the same steps for the Bip01 L Hand object so that it rotates off the heel.

Continue Setting Keys

Next we'll work with the pivot points to animate the left foot taking off from the ground at frame 20. We'll do this by starting the foot rotation at frame 15. In order to do this, we will need an additional key at frame 10.

1. Select the left foot.

2. Go to frame 10.

3. Click [icon] Set Planted Key.

4. Go to frame 15.

5. Click [icon] Set Planted Key.

   This fixes the foot pivot point at this frame.

   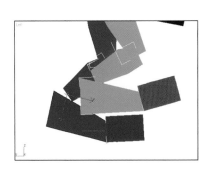

6. On frame 15, rotate the foot upward slightly.

   The pivot point is at the ball of the foot, which is just fine. Now we want to animate the foot pivot at the tips of the toes as it takes off from the ground.

7. Go to frame 20.

8. Click Select Pivot. We need to set a new pivot location at this frame.

9. Set the pivot to the tips of the toes.

10. Turn off Select Pivot.

11. Rotate the foot.

The foot rotates from the middle despite the new pivot point.

Sliding Keys

For the type of movement we want for the dog's leg, a *sliding key* is needed. This allows the foot to move around while still retaining some of the characteristics of a planted key, such as staying still when the COM is moved.

1. With the left foot selected, click [icon] Set Sliding Key.

Notice that the Join to Prev IK Key checkbox is now cleared, meaning the foot isn't locked to the previous key's position.

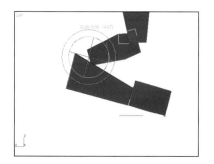

2. Rotate the foot upward.

The foot now rotates from the toe. (In the image shown here, the right foot has been hidden for clarity.)

Scrub between frames 0 and 10 now, and you'll see that even though the keys are the same on those frames, the left-rear heel dips slightly below the ground between these frames. This is because the foot "drifts" between keyframes.

3. Go to frame 0.

4. With the left foot selected, expand the TCB section. Set the Tension parameter in the Key Info rollout to 50. Don't confuse this Tension setting with the Ankle Tension setting found in the IK section, they're two different parameters.

5. Go to frame 10.

6. Set the Tension parameter to 50.

The foot no longer drifts between frames 0 and 10.

►NOTE◄

In 3ds Max version 8, you now change the Tension, Bias, and Continuity settings by adjusting the biped's function curves in Track View - Curve Editor. You'll learn more about this in Chapter 8.

With the techniques you have learned here so far, you can now make a freeform character do just about anything.

EXERCISE 7.5

Jumping Dog

In this exercise, you'll practice combining freeform techniques to make the dog jump and wag its tail.

1. Load the file `HappyDogJumpStart.max` from the CD.

   This file contains the dog doing a goofy walk, then stopping and bowing its head. We're going to make the dog jump.

2. Hide the named selection set `Dog Parts`. The biped remains visible in the viewport.

3. Go to frame 80.

   The last frame of the animation is on frame 80. We don't want the dog's hands and feet (all four paws) to start moving until after this frame, so we need to set some planted keys at frame 80.

4. For each hand and foot, click 🔲 Set Planted Key.

   Now we'll begin to animate the jump. The front of the body will come up first, followed by the back end.

5. Go to frame 90.

6. For each of the back feet, click 🔲 Set Planted Key.

7. For each of the hands, click 🔲 Set Free Key.

   This will allow the front paws to leave the ground.

8. Turn on the Auto Key button.

   Although you could just continue using the Set Key buttons to do all the keyframing, using Auto Key will make it go a little more quickly.

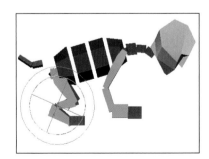

9. Rotate each of the back feet so that the heels move upward.

10. Move the COM upward and forward.

11. Rotate the lowest spine link (the one closest to the COM) to tilt the body upward. Rotate each of the spine links to add curvature to the dog's spine. Notice that the rear feet stay planted on the ground, but the front feet leave the ground and move with the body.

12. Rotate the arms (the dog's front legs) forward and outward.

13. Rotate the head to look upward.

14. Click Body Rotation, and click Set Key.

    This completes the necessary movement of the dog so far.

Checking the Animation of the Mesh

To see how the animation is shaping up, it can be helpful to unhide the dog parts.

1. Select the named selection set Dog Parts.

    This unhides and selects the dog parts.

2. On the Display panel, in the Display Properties rollout, check the See-Through checkbox.

    This makes all the dog parts see-through. Now you can see the dog as you work with the biped.

3. On the Display panel, expand the Freeze rollout and click Freeze Selected.

    Now you can see the mesh objects, but you won't be able to select them by accident.

4. Go to frame 95.

5. For each of the back feet, click ☒ Set Free Key so that the back feet will be able to leave the ground.

6. Use the COM to move and rotate the dog upward and forward, as if it were airborne. Of course, all four paws will now move with the COM.

7. Rotate the head to face it forward.

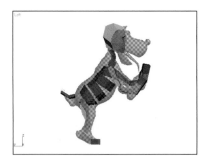

►TIP◄
Use the Page Down key to move down the hierarchy, such as the spine links.

8. Rotate the toes to straighten them out. You can also rotate the legs outward a little to make the jump more comical.

   Look to see whether the feet automatically go with the legs when you rotate them outward—if they don't, you'll have to rotate the feet separately. (This might be a bug; 3ds Max behaves differently on various video graphics cards. If it happens to you, just work around it by rotating the feet separately.)

9. For each paw that you don't actually animate, click Set Free Key.

Animating the Landing

Now for the landing. To make the dog land on the same plane that he was walking on earlier, you can place a box object at frame 90, before the dog takes off.

1. Go to frame 100.

2. Move the COM downward and forward to make the dog's front paws hit the ground.

   It's OK if the feet don't hit simultaneously; in fact, it will look more realistic if their landing doesn't exactly match. Matched action is called "twinning" in classical animation and is to be avoided.

3. Rotate and move the hands (front feet) and the COM to position the heels of the hands so they hit the ground before the fingers during the landing. Moving the hands will make the "elbows" bend on impact, looking more lifelike.

4. Tilt the head upward.

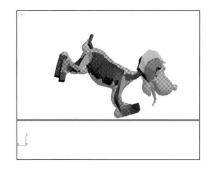

   Notice that if you don't animate the head, it will look unnatural (when we move, all our parts move; none stays stock still). The rotation of the head seems to counterbalance the movement of the body and limbs.

5. For each hand, click Set Planted Key to fix both of them in space.

6. Go to frame 110.

7. Rotate and move the COM, spine, and legs to tuck the biped's legs underneath it, as shown in the figure. This creates the natural motion of the dog's body following through the arc of motion of the leap.

   While you're tucking the feet under the body, the biped might appear to get all tangled up. This is normal. The hands (front paws) are staying put, so you'll have to rotate the COM, spine, and legs any way you can in order to get the legs underneath the body.

8. For each hand and foot, click ![icon] Set Planted Key.

9. If necessary, rotate the fingers to flatten them on the ground. You may need to set the pivot point to the heel of the hand to make this step easier.

10. Rotate the biped's head downward as a natural response to the landing.

11. Go to frame 125.

12. Position the dog in its final sitting position by moving the COM downward, rotating the lowest spine link upward, and tilting the head upward.

Animating the Tail

All the dog needs now is a wagging tail. The tail can be animated just like any other body part.

1. Select both tail links.

2. Move to frame 20. Rotate the tail links to wag the tail to one side.

3. Continue moving ahead 5 or 10 frames at a time, and animate the rotation of the entire tail.

   Try to time the tail movement so it naturally follows the rising and falling of the dog's hindquarters. When the dog's COM drops to its lowest point, animate the tail rotation downward 5 frames after that. (In classical animation this is called *secondary motion* or *follow-through*.) Continue this process until you reach frame 125.

If you like, you can eliminate the wagging during the airborne period.

4. Hide the biped and unfreeze the dog parts. Select the dog parts and turn off See-through on Object Properties. The animation is now complete.

5. Render or play the animation. The dog walks, jumps, and wags its tail.

A finished version of this animation can be found in the file `HappyDogJumpFinal.max` on the CD.

Freeform Between Footsteps

Suppose you want your character to run for a few steps before taking off and flying in the air, then land and take a few more steps. If you simply set up footsteps and make the biped airborne while it's supposed to be flying, the biped will bounce high into the air and can't be brought down again (as you saw in the Chapter 5 exercise "Leapin' Biped"). This happens because the airborne period is under the control of gravity, and subject to the calculations of the footstep method of animation.

What you can do to accomplish this sort of animation is set up a *freeform period* during the airborne time between the starting and ending footsteps. During a freeform period between footsteps, gravity is suspended and the biped won't go flying up into the air, even though it has plenty of airborne time. In a freeform period between footsteps, the biped simply drifts from the previous footstep key to the next one, leaving you free to animate the biped any way you want to during those frames.

To use freeform animation in this way, the freeform period must have footsteps both before and after it. However, you can set up a freeform period during any airborne period between footsteps.

To set up a freeform period within footsteps, open the Track View - Dope Sheet and right-click anywhere in the footstep key display. In the Bip01 Footstep Mode dialog, select "Edit Free Form (no physics)". You'll see a hollow yellow outline around all areas in the footstep key display that can be turned into freeform areas.

To make the freeform area, click inside the yellow outline. The box will turn solid yellow; all keys for the biped during that period are removed, and you can animate the biped in any way you like. To change a freeform period back into a gravity period, click the yellow box again to turn it into an outline.

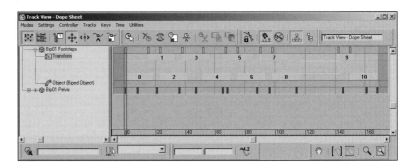

EXERCISE 7.6

A Refreshing Swim

In this exercise, we'll use a freeform period between footsteps to make a biped swim.

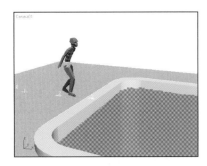

1. Load the file Dive.max from the CD and play the animation.

   This file contains a footstep animation at a swimming pool. The camera follows the biped as it runs for the pool, then leaps to jump in. After a few moments, the biped ascends the steps at the end of the pool.

   Because the entire animation is a footstep animation, gravity is in effect, and the biped jumps very high into the air during the period when it should be swimming. In order to make the biped jump into the pool and swim to the steps, you'll make this period a freeform period.

2. Open Track View - Dope Sheet and display the footstep keys.

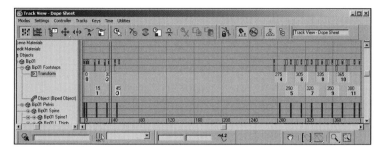

3. Right-click anywhere in the footstep key area.

   The Bip01 Footstep Mode dialog appears.

4. Choose "Edit Free Form (no physics)."

5. Click on the large yellow box outline at the center of the footstep key area.

   The box becomes solid yellow, indicating that this is now a freeform period.

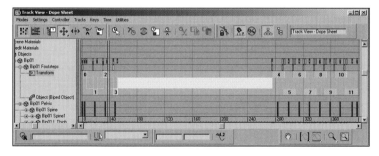

6. Close the Bip01 Footstep Mode dialog, and minimize the Dope Sheet.

7. Play the animation.

   The biped now "floats" during the freeform period.

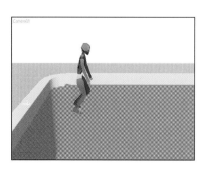

Make the Biped Dive

You can now animate the biped during the freeform period you have established.

1. Go to frame 51.

   This is the last frame of the footstep animation. Here you'll prepare the biped for the dive into the pool.

2. Turn on Auto Key.

   The biped is now in a freeform period.

3. Bend the biped over, and swing its arms behind its back to prepare for the jump. Also, move the COM downward to bend the right knee, and bend the left leg next to it.

4. Go to frame 65. Pose the biped in mid-dive.

5. Go to frame 80. Pose the biped in a diving position, with its body about halfway in the water.

6. Go to frame 90, and move the biped deeper into the pool.

7. Go to frame 100, and rotate the COM to show the biped starting to turn toward the surface.

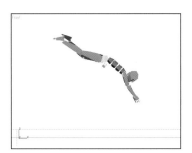
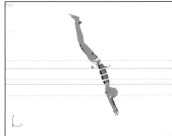
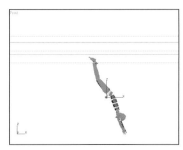
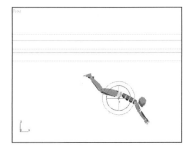

Keep the Biped from Moving

During the freeform period, the biped will continually move toward its keyframes at the start of the next footstep period. This can be frustrating when you're trying to animate the swimming portion of the animation. To correct this situation, you'll go to a frame near the end of the freeform period and put the biped in a swimming pose. Use the Copy/Paste Posture tools to copy the biped's entire pose from one frame to another.

1. On frame 100, select the entire biped. In the Copy/Paste roll-out, click ⬚ Create Collection.

2. In the Copy Collections field, name the collection swim collection. In the Copied Postures group, click ⬚ Capture Snapshot from Viewport.

3. Activate the Front viewport; then press the P key to turn it into a Perspective viewport.

4. On the Tools menu, choose Isolate Selection and then click ⬚ Copy Posture.

   The copied posture appears in the Copied Postures list, and a thumbnail of the posture is visible in the window. You can exit Isolation mode after doing this. The biped was isolated just so you could get the biped unobstructed in the thumbnail.

5. Go to frame 200, and click ⬚ Paste Posture.

6. Rotate and/or move the COM as necessary to put the biped in a swimming pose.

   Now when you return to earlier frames, the biped won't be trying to stand up.

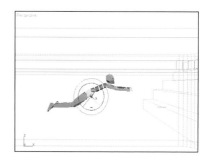

7. Continue to animate the biped between frames 100 and 200, adding arm and leg movements to make it swim.

   You can see a finished version of this exercise in the file Swim.max on the CD.

Converting Freeform to Footsteps

Generally, once you've created a purely freeform animation, you can no longer place footsteps in the scene. However, if your freeform animation meets certain rules, you can convert it to footstep animation and then edit the footstep sequence as usual.

Only freeform areas that resemble footsteps can be converted to footsteps. Your freeform animation must have places where a foot has IK Blend set to 1 and Object selected—which, as you saw with the walking dog, simulates the action of a footstep icon.

To convert a freeform animation to footsteps, select any part of the biped and go to the Motion panel. In the Biped rollout, click Convert. When the Convert to Footsteps dialog appears, check the box for Flatten Footsteps to Z = 0. Now, wherever a foot has an IK Blend value of 1 and Object selected, a footstep will be created for that foot. (Footsteps are never created for hands, even if the IK Blend is 1 and Object is selected.)

In Chapter 6, "Advanced Footsteps," we converted footsteps into freeform; now that you know how to do the reverse, you can convert back and forth between freeform and footstep animation as often as you like during an animation.

In both types of conversion, you have the option to generate a keyframe per frame. This can be a good idea when you want to maintain all the nuances of the animation. Otherwise, you might lose some of the upper body animation (which we'll get into in the next chapter). Experiment with in your own animations and see what works best for you.

►NOTE◄

All footsteps will be created on the XY construction plane. This is fine if the biped was animated on this plane, but not so good if it wasn't.

CHAPTER 8

Body Animation

When you use the footstep animation workflow, you place and time footsteps as accurately as possible, and then you move on to animating the rest of the body. The default keys created for the upper body in footstep animation are limited to a slight swaying of the hips, spine, arms, and head. The creators of Character Studio expected that no one would leave the upper body animation like this, but would add many more movements to bring the character to life.

Because your biped already has keys, however, to continue its enhancement you'll need a good understanding of the many tools available for working with keys. Otherwise, you might put new keys too close to existing keys, causing the biped to jerk and spasm as it moves through the keys.

Working with Keys

Sometimes it's easiest to convert your footstep animation into freeform animation using the Convert button, and then continue animating using freeform. You begin with footsteps to solve the problem of creating convincing foot-to-ground contact, and then use freeform for the rest of your animation.

It's important to remember that you must get the footstep placement and timing as close to perfect as possible before attempting to work with the rest of the body. This is necessary because keys for the body are reset every time you create keys for inactive footsteps. If you've done any work on the upper body, and then you deactivate footsteps and create keys for them again, all the keys for the body will be reset and you'll lose the work you've done on the body.

There are several tools you can use to set and edit keys for the biped's upper body. In some cases, these tools differ from the ones you use with ordinary 3ds Max objects.

Track View

In Track View - Dope Sheet you can see the keys that are automatically created by footsteps for the hips, spine, and arms. (A *track* is simply a slot that goes across in time from the start of the animation to the end.) Right-click any of these biped objects and choose Dope Sheet to navigate directly to their keys. They are represented by color-coded key dots: red for position, green for rotation, and blue for scale. There are quite a number of dots for each biped.

With ordinary 3ds Max objects, you're accustomed to seeing tracks such as Position, Rotation, and Scale for each object. Character Studio objects, however, generally have only one track, called Transform. This track can be expanded to reveal the Biped Sub-Anim track, which includes three List Controller tracks for Position, Rotation, and Scale. Here in the Biped Sub-Anim track you can add as many controller tracks as you like. The various tracks can be weighted to layer their animation effect.

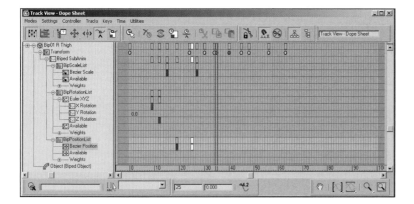

Whether you move, rotate, or scale the body part, it will appear on the Transform track. One Transform track key holds all the position, rotation, and scale information.

Function Curves in Biped

In ordinary 3ds Max animation, you've most likely encountered a situation where an object "drifts" a little between keys even though both keys are the same. This can also happen with freeform animation, where the foot or hand drifts a little between planted keys. In 3ds Max you generally solve this problem in Track View - Curve Editor, by adjusting function curves to straight lines going into or out of keys. New to 3ds Max 8, function curves are available for editing your biped motions. In previous versions, this task was difficult because biped objects are animated using Quaternion (tension, continuity, and bias, or "TCB") controllers, which aren't displayed the same way as Euler XYZ rotation controllers.

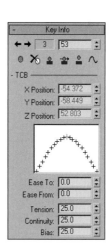

If you leave the default TCB rotations selected, you can use the Tension, Continuity, and Bias parameters on the Key Info rollout to keep a hand or foot from drifting. The effects of changing these values can be observed in the TCB graph on the Key Info rollout.

The proximity of X marks on the TCB graph tell you the relative speed of the motion into or out of the key: X's far apart indicate faster motion, X's close together mean slower motion.

You can use any of the following settings to simulate a straight-line function curve for a key:

- Changing Bias to 0 or 50 causes a straight line going *either* into or out of a key.

- Changing both Bias and Continuity to 0 causes a straight line going into *and* out of the key.

- Changing Tension to 50, just like changing Bias and Continuity to 0, causes a straight line going both into *and* out of the key.

Animators trained in Maya or SoftImage are accustomed to adjusting their character animation using function curves. Although the Workbench (available in versions of Character Studio 4 and later) was an attempt to provide this type of tool, 3ds Max 8 represents a significant improvement, offering function curves for both Quaternion and Euler controllers for biped objects.

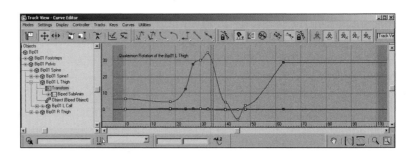

Quaternion controllers calculate a single value from a matrix (chart of values). Euler controllers, on the other hand, calculate three separate values for XYZ rotation. Because the second two of these calculations are based on the first, Euler controllers allow for the additional control of specifying the order of axis calculation. Any controller keys can be switched from Quaternion (the default) to Euler by simply using the radio buttons in the Quaternion/Euler rollout on the Motion panel. Keys can be changed back and forth as needed. 3ds Max tries its best to maintain the function curve in such a way that shifting between the two types of curves does not significantly affect the motion.

Quaternion controllers display function curves that let you move the keys and edit their interpolation. Another advantage of Euler controllers is that they display tangent handles for key interpolation adjustment. If you're familiar with drawing splines in 3ds Max or in any vector drawing program, you're probably accustomed to using tangent handles to adjust curves.

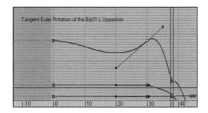

You can edit your animation by viewing the curves and looking for spikes and other anomalies. You can see the effect in real time in the viewport as the object rotations update with the release of the mouse button in the Track View - Curve Editor.

Another improvement to the Track View - Curve Editor is separate tracks for the keys for the components of the arms and legs. Even the fingers have their own track curves—now only the finger links lack their own individual track curves.

Since 3ds Max allows you to place a Sound Track in Track View, you can now very easily synchronize finger movements to music in animations of characters playing musical instruments.

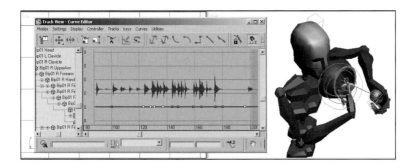

Adding or Changing Keys

A couple of special rules apply to biped body keys created with footsteps:

- Some keys appear in Dope Sheet as red dots. You'll notice that the red keys align with the beginnings and ends of footsteps.

These red keys can't be moved or deleted. However, any other keys can be moved or deleted.

- Biped keys often cannot be cloned, particularly when footstep animation is being used. To get around this, you can copy the posture and paste it to another key (as described later in this chapter).

For changing or adding a key to the upper body, conventional 3ds Max tools are used. As you learned in Chapter 7, you can accomplish quite a bit simply by turning on Auto Key and posing your character at various frames. Alternatively, you can move a body part and then click Set Key on the Key Info rollout to set the key only for the currently selected body part on the current frame.

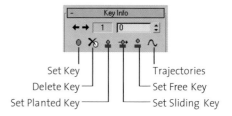

Also in the Key Info rollout you'll find other Set Key buttons that will be familiar from Chapter 7. Set Planted Key lets you anchor the foot or hands in space at any given frame; it also lets you keyframe the pivot point for the hands or feet. Set Sliding Key works similarly, but you can move the hand or foot away from the pivot point in space. These are very handy tools, because you can lock the position of the hand or foot in space with the selected pivot and then reposition the upper body or COM to animate the limbs.

To animate the arms, you can also use ⊕ Select and Move to pick up a hand and move it directly. The arm will rotate accordingly because IK is automatically built into the biped model for the hands and, to some degree, the feet. Since the entire arm's animation is on multiple tracks in Track View - Dope Sheet, using

►QUICKLIST◄

FREEFORM ANIMATING

1. Turn off Footstep mode if it's still on.
2. Go to a frame other than 0.
3. Click Select and Rotate.
4. Turn on Auto Key.
5. Move or rotate the arms, hands, spine, and neck links as you like.

►NOTE◄

The Set Key and other key buttons are available only when you are not in Footstep mode.

►TIP◄

Remember, you can't position the pivot point just anywhere. Character Studio gives you a choice among various locations represented by dots on the hands or feet.

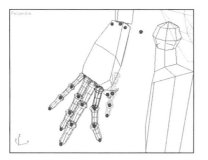

Select and Move in the viewport will set a key for each of the objects in the entire arm. After moving the hand or foot, you can rotate it into the correct position.

In previous versions of Biped, the pelvis animation was hard-wired to the COM and so could only be rotated by rotating the root biped object. New to 3ds Max 8 is the ability to rotate the pelvis in three degrees of freedom. If you rotate the pelvis, the rotation will also affect the leg objects.

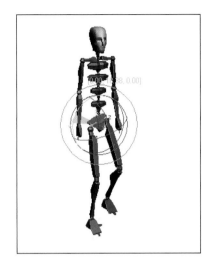

Although in 3ds Max 8 you can now rotate the pelvis, you can't animate it using Select and Move to create position keys; you must still move the COM to animate the pelvis.

Working with Existing Keys

As with ordinary 3ds Max animation, if you put new keys too close to existing keys, the biped will jerk and spasm as it moves through the keys. So when adding more upper-body animation to the biped, you have two choices for this process:

- You can change only frames that already have keys, overwriting the existing keys.

- You can delete all the keys and make new ones.

To change only existing keys, you have to know where the keys are. There are two ways to find out: Look in Track View, or use Key Mode Toggle.

For the first method, open Track View (either the Dope Sheet or Curve Editor, as you like) and locate the track you want to animate. Click on individual keys and note their frame numbers displayed at the bottom of the Track View window. In addition, take note of areas where there are no keys for 10 frames or more. These are areas where you can safely add more keys without ruining the animation.

To use the Key Mode Toggle method of finding the keys, select the body part you want to animate in a viewport and turn on ⏮⏭ Key Mode Toggle. Use the ▶| Next Key and |◀ Previous Key buttons to move from one keyframe to the next. This is standard practice for all Max animation—it helps you avoid setting keys without forethought, and it can also help you avoid setting keys too close together.

If you choose to delete all existing keys and make new ones, open Track View - Dope Sheet and locate the track. Select keys and press the Delete key, and the selected keys will be deleted.

You can also use the Dope Sheet Time tools, specifically Select Time and Delete Time, as another way to delete keys.

And finally, you can delete a key for a particular body part right in the Motion panel. Select the body part, move to the key's frame, and click ✗ Delete Key on the Key Info rollout.

EXERCISE 8.1

Animating Arms

In this first exercise, we'll animate the arms of the jumping biped. We'll use the Key Mode Toggle method to place the keys. First, we'll take a look at the existing keys for the arms, so that we know where it's safe to add a key.

1. Load the file `Jump.max` from this book's CD.

    This file contains a biped doing an eight-footstep jump. The default jump is somewhat lackluster. We'll spruce it up with some arm motion.

2. Select both the left and right upper arms.

    Look at the trackbar at the bottom of the screen to see the existing keys for the arms. These keys were generated when keys were created for the footsteps.

3. Right-click and choose Dope Sheet.

4. Scroll down in the Dope Sheet object list to find the keys for
   `Bip01`. Expand the hierarchy, if necessary, to view the keys for
   the biped.

5. Locate and highlight the Transform tracks under Bip01 L Clavicle and Bip01 R Clavicle.

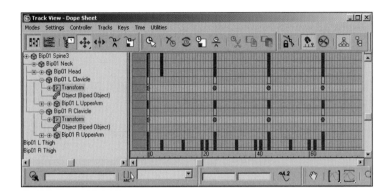

6. Click on a few of the keys on these tracks. Notice the keys'
   frame numbers in the Key Stats: Track View toolbar at the
   bottom of the Dope Sheet window.

   Notice that there are no keys in the area of frame 20. This
   means we can place a new key there without making the
   biped jerk and spasm.

7. Close the Dope Sheet.

Add New Keys

1. Go to frame 20.

2. Turn on the Auto Key button.

3. In the Left viewport, rotate the biped's upper arms on the Z
   axis slightly behind the body to prepare for the jump.

4. In the Track Selection rollout, click [⟳] Body Rotation.

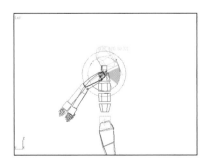

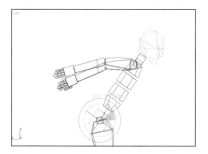

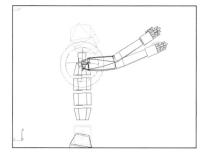

5. Rotate the body forward by about 35 degrees to prepare for the jump.

6. Select both of the upper arms.

7. Turn on 🔾 Key Mode Toggle.

8. Click the ▶️ Next Key button to move to the next arm key, at frame 25.

9. Rotate both upper arms upward to propel the biped forward for the jump. This automatically overwrites the existing arm keys at frame 25.

10. Play the animation. The biped now uses its arms to prepare for the second jump.

11. Save the scene with the filename Arms.max.

Copying and Pasting Postures

As mentioned earlier, sometimes Character Studio won't let you clone a key, so you'll need to copy the posture and paste it to a new key. This technique has many other uses, as well, in animating. It can save you time in keyframing. For example, after you get the right arm correct for frame 15 in a walk cycle, you can Paste Opposite to get the left arm correct at frame 20. Also, many animators build up a library of arm/leg/body positions that they can then copy and paste as needed in their animations. And copy and paste is also useful when creating a looping animation, since the first and last keys must be identical to avoid jumping every time the loop repeats.

The posture of any body part can be copied to another frame using the 🔾 Copy Posture, 🔾 Paste Posture, and 🔾 Paste Posture Opposite buttons, found on the Copy/Paste rollout.

When you click Copy Posture, the posture of the selected body part is copied into memory. Paste Posture pastes the most recently copied posture to the currently selected body part. Paste Posture Opposite pastes the copied posture to the opposite side of the body, and only works when an arm or leg posture has been copied.

►NOTE◄

In 3ds Max 8, you must first create a Copy Collection using the Create Collection button before you can copy or paste any postures. In order for a pasted posture to "stick," either Auto Key must be on when you paste the posture, or you must click Set Key after pasting the posture.

EXERCISE 8.2

Copy and Paste Arm Postures

In this exercise, you'll continue animating the jumping biped's arms. Here, you'll use Copy Posture and Paste Posture to copy the positions of the arm keys from one frame to another.

1. Load the file Arms.max that you made in the preceding exercise, or load the file from the CD.

2. Go to frame 20.

   This is where the arms swing back to prepare for the jump.

3. Activate the Perspective viewport, then select the biped's upper arms and the COM.

4. On the Copy/Paste rollout, click 🔳 Create Collection. Turn on 🔲 Capture Snapshot from Viewport—the leftmost icon below the Copied Postures window.

5. Click 🔳 Copy Posture.

   The arm and COM postures have been copied. A thumbnail is displayed in the Copied Postures window.

6. Go to frame 40.

7. Turn on the Auto Key button.

8. Click 🔳 Paste Posture.

   The biped's arm and COM positions are pasted to frame 40, and keys are set for them. (You may need to rotate the lowest spine link, if the COM position isn't pasted.)

9. Go to frame 25.

   Here, the biped's arms are raised to propel it into the air.

10. Select both upper arms and, if necessary, right-click the Perspective viewport to activate it.

11. Click 🔳 Copy Posture.

12. Go to frame 45.

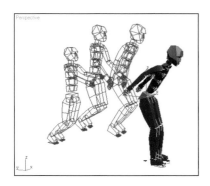

13. Click [icon] Paste Posture.

14. Play the animation.

    The biped now prepares for the second and third jumps by bending over and putting its arms behind its body, and then swings its arms forward to propel it upward for the jump.

15. Save the scene with the filename Armsup.max.

Working with Layers

Layers for animation are not a standard tool in 3ds Max. There is a Layers functionality in 3ds Max, but this is a CAD-based system that is used primarily to hide and unhide sets of objects. Layers for animation are unique to Character Studio and are not yet available for standard 3ds Max objects.

Essentially, layers let you take an existing animation and then, by creating a new animation layer, add new animation that can be made active or turned off. This gives you the opportunity to try out various ideas. It's ideal for adding more animation to motion capture files, especially when there are lots and lots of keyframes to contend with.

Layers can be used to separate different types of animation so that they can be viewed and edited separately. For example, all the animation for the arms can be on one layer, while another layer holds the head or spine animation. Or, suppose you have a motion capture file of a character running; you could add a layer on the Body Rotation track to make the biped run upside-down on the ceiling.

All the usual animation features, such as copying and pasting postures, work with layers. In general, when using layers, you animate the same way as always. Layers just give you more control over the animation, allowing you to view certain parts of the motion and keep them separate for easier editing.

Keep in mind that you can only access layers when Footstep mode is turned off. Layers can only be used to animate upper-body motion, not footstep motion (which is always part of the Original layer).

Layers are controlled with the Layers rollout in the Motion panel. By default, a layer called Original is created to hold the footstep animation, as well as any animation you have created without layers.

To create a layer, expand the Layers rollout and click Create Layer; then enter a name for the layer. Animate any part of the biped. As you animate, a red skeleton shows you the original position of the biped for reference. You can use the Biped Set Key button or the Auto Key method to create the layer keyframes. If you want to add some motion but you don't want it on that layer, you'll need to create another layer to hold the motion.

Click Create Layer again to create another layer for a different part or parts of the body. In the Layers rollout, click the large black up or down arrows to move up and down between layers. Go to the highest layer when you want to use all layers.

The 🔘 Snap Set Key button resets the selected body parts to the body position on the Original layer. This can be handy for pasting a posture from the Original layer into the current layer.

Generally, you will get the best results by collapsing the layers when you're satisfied with your animation. You may need to leave them uncollapsed for a project that experiences frequent changes, but usually the workflow is best served by collapsing the layers after you've made the edits you need.

EXERCISE 8.3

Animating with Layers

In this exercise, you'll animate the arms of a dancing biped. This will let you try out various arm motions using a nondestructive workflow method.

1. Load the file Dance_Start.max from the CD.

This file contains a biped doing a simple dance about 260 frames long.

2. Select any part of the biped.

3. Turn off Footstep mode, if it's on.

    We want to animate the arms for the dance. We'll start by removing all the existing arm keys.

4. Open Track View - Dope Sheet, and expand the hierarchy to view all the biped keys.

5. Locate the `Bip01 L Clavicle` and `Bip01 R Clavicle` tracks.

6. Highlight the Transform tracks for both Bipo1 L Clavicle and Bipo1 R Clavicle.

7. Select all the keys in both clavicle Transform tracks.

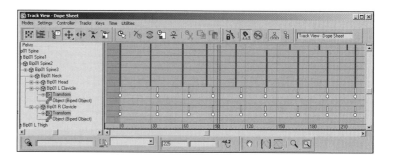

8. Press the Delete key on the keyboard.

    All the clavicle keys in the Dope Sheet window disappear. The arm keys are deleted.

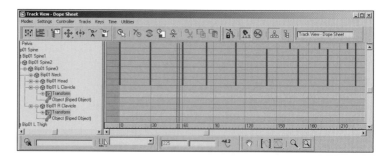

9. Close Track View.

Create a Layer

Now we're ready to use layers and begin animating.

1. Select any part of the biped.

2. Expand the Layers rollout.

3. Click Create Layer.

4. In the entry area, enter the name Arms.

5. Turn on the Auto Key button.

6. Go to frame 35.

   This is the frame where the biped's right foot steps outward to begin the dance. Here, we want to make the arms come up to a bent position on this first step.

7. Bend the biped's left arm and hand upward, as shown.

   The red skeleton shows the original position of the biped's arm. As you rotate the arm, the red skeleton doesn't change.

►TIP◄

As always in 3ds Max, for an entry in a list you should use names that you can easily identify and return to.

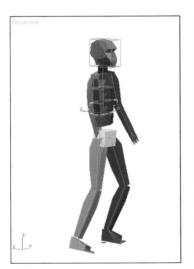
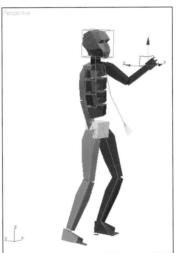

8. Select the entire left arm and hand.

9. Click Create Collection, then Copy Posture, and then 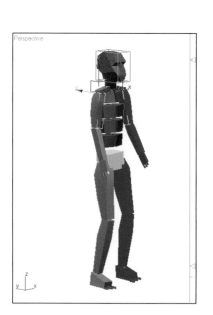 Paste Posture Opposite.

   The animation is pasted to the other arm.

10. Scroll the time slider back and forth.

    Whoops! We forgot to set keys on frame 0 for the arms.

Snap Set Key

No problem—we can use the Snap Set Key feature to position the arms in their original pose for frame 0. Remember, the default Original layer holds the starting positions for every biped object. Then we can simply paste the arm positions and use Snap Set Key to set up the remainder of the arm motion for the dance.

1. Go to frame 0.

2. Select both upper arms.

3. In the Layers rollout, click ⬚ Snap Set Key.

   The arms are forced back to the pose they hold on the Original layer, and a key is set.

4. Go to frame 35.

5. Select both arms and both hands.

6. Click Copy Posture.

7. Go to frame 65, and click ⬚ Snap Set Key.

8. Go to frame 90, and click ⬚ Paste Posture.

9. Continue using Snap Set Key and Paste Posture for these frames:

Frame	Pose
120	Snap Set Key
145	Paste Posture
160	Snap Set Key

Frame	Pose
175	Paste Posture
188	Snap Set Key
200	Paste Posture
213	Snap Set Key

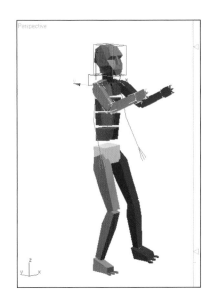

10. Play the animation.

    The biped now moves its arms up and down in sync with the foot motions and jumping.

Refine the Dance

Now you'll add a few more keys to make the dance look even better. You'll also create an additional layer for the head animation.

1. On frame 10, click ⚙ Snap Set Key.

    This keeps the biped's arms down for a few more frames before they start to move upward for the dance.

2. On frames 50 and 100, click 📋 Paste Posture.

    This keeps the biped's arms up for a few more frames.

3. In the Layers rollout, click Create Layer.

    Now we'll animate the biped's head in a new layer. There are no keys on the head, so there's no need to delete keys before animating. This gives you the opportunity to try out the head animation. If you don't like it, set the layer to inactive so that it's not used but not destroyed.

4. In the entry area, enter the name Head.

    Notice that the red skeleton displays the pose of the previous (Original) layer.

5. Animate the head turning to the left and right as the biped moves through the dance.

6. Continue adding layers and animating as you like. For example, you can animate the spine bending to the left, right, backward, or forward at various times.

You can see a finished version of this dance in the file `Dance_Finish.max` on the CD.

Using Apply Increment

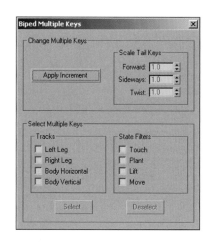

There may be times when you want to adjust a biped body part throughout the entire animation. This can be accomplished with the Apply Increment feature.

To use this feature, first use the trackbar to select the keys you want to change. Then click ⊞ Set Multiple Keys on the Keyframing Tools rollout to display the Biped Multiple Keys dialog.

Make a change to a body part, then click Apply Increment. The change will be applied to all selected keys.

Be careful not to apply the same change twice to the original keyframe! If you do this, the original key will be incremented twice, giving you unexpected results.

EXERCISE 8.4

Adjusting Arms

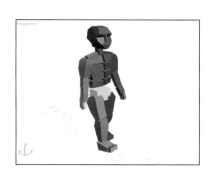

In this exercise, we'll make a stocky biped move its arms away from its body. We'll use the Apply Increment feature to change the arms throughout the animation so that the biped flaps its arms like a chicken trying to take flight.

1. Load the file `Stocky.max` from the CD.

This file contains a stocky biped with an eight-footstep walk. The biped walks with its arms at its sides.

2. Select the biped's right and left UpperArm objects.

3. Go to frame 0.

   In the trackbar, you'll see the biped keys for the arms.

4. On the Keyframing Tools rollout, click [icon] Set Multiple Keys.

   The Biped Multiple Keys dialog appears. You might need to move the dialog to another part of the screen so you can see it and the Front viewport at the same time.

5. In the trackbar, select every other key for the arms from frame 30 onward.

6. In the Front viewport, rotate the left and right arms on their Y axes until the arms sit away from the body.

   Rotate each arm, whether separately or together, only once. If you don't do it correctly the first time, undo and rotate again.

7. Immediately after rotating each arm, click Apply Increment. Click this button only once, even if it looks as though nothing happened.

   The rotation has been applied to all selected arm keys.

8. Play the animation, and you'll see how all the selected arm keys have been affected. The stocky biped flaps its arms like a chicken.

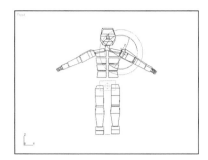

►NOTE◄

You might see something strange happening onscreen—the biped arms might have become disengaged from the rest of the body. This is simply a display problem that sometimes occurs with Character Studio; the animation is actually fine. If you move the time slider to another frame, the arms will snap back into place.

►NOTE◄

Any animation sequence—footstep, upper body, or freeform—can be saved in a **BIP** file. This file can be loaded onto any biped to make it perform the same motions you have set up in the animation. To save a **BIP** file, in the Motion panel, click Save File on the Biped rollout. To load a **BIP** file onto a biped, click Load File and choose any **BIP** file. After a few moments, the motion is loaded and the biped changes position. Play the animation to see the motion.

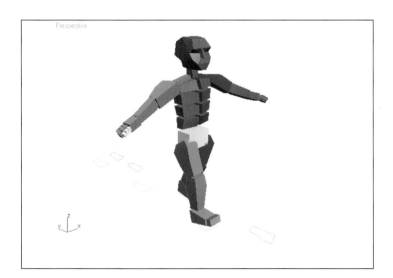

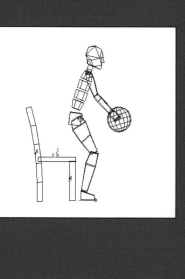

CHAPTER 9

Arms and Hands

A biped's arms and hands have special features that ordinary bones don't have. Joint limits are preset on certain biped bones to correspond to those of the human body and can't be changed. For instance, you can't rotate the lower part of your leg in certain directions or you will break it, and the same is true with biped skeletons.

Biped hand and feet objects allow you to set planted keys on pivot points and then shift the location of the pivot points. This makes it easy to do heel-to-toe rolling movements on feet, and similar hand movements, as well.

You can link objects to the biped's hands (as you can to any body part) to make the objects move with the hands. Conversely, you can cause the biped's hands to follow another object's animation, by using IK Blend.

On both the arms and the legs, you can cause bulges to appear in the character's skin based on the bend angle between two adjacent biped bones. For example, when a character bends its elbow, you can make a bicep bulge appear in the upper arm.

Linking Objects to the Biped

To make the biped pick up an object, the process is quite straight-forward. You simply link the object to another stationary object at first, and then use the *Link Constraint controller* to link the object to the biped's hand at the appropriate moment.

Link Constraint allows an object to be linked to one object at first and then to be linked to another object at a specific frame. Although Link Constraint is a standard 3ds Max tool and not really part of Character Studio, this tool is needed so often by animators, that we have included an exercise for this object-linking procedure. (More information on Link Constraint is available in the 3ds Max manuals and online help.)

EXERCISE 9.1

Picking Up a Ball

In this exercise, you'll make a biped bend over and pick up a ball, by changing what the ball is linked to.

1. Load the file `Standing.max` from the CD. This file contains a biped standing up from a sitting position.

2. Go to frame 50.

3. Turn on the Auto Key button.

4. Select the Biped and open the Motion panel. On the Track Selection rollout, click ↕ Body Vertical to select the correct COM track.

5. In the Left viewport, move the COM downward until the biped's hips are almost touching the chair. Then select the ↔ Body Horizontal track and slide it until the biped shifts a little away from the back of the chair.

6. Rotate the biped's spine, arms, and head to bend the biped over into a position where it can pick up the ball.

> ►TIP◄
>
> Character Studio in 3ds Max 8 has both Quaternion and Euler controllers available. If you get unexpected results with Balance Factor, especially when loading older files, try switching the COM to Euler controller. Do this in the Quaternion/Euler rollout in the Motion panel.

Notice that when you rotate the biped's spine, the entire biped makes adjustments due to Balance Factor. To fix this do the following: Select the Body Rotation track, then in the Key Info rollout click the Set Key button to set a key. Expand the Body section, click the Body Horizontal Track, and change the Balance Factor to 0.

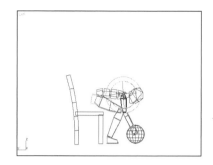

7. In the Front viewport, position the biped's hands so they're touching the ball.

8. Go to frame 70.

9. Move the biped back into a standing position. Place its arms slightly in front of the body, where the ball will be held.

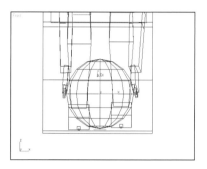

   The biped now bends over at frame 50 and then stands up again.

Link the Ball

Your next task is to make the ball "stick" to one of the biped's hands at frame 50, using Link Constraint. You could stick both hands to the ball if you wanted to, but you'd still have to keyframe it one hand at a time.

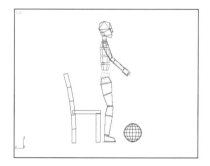

1. Select the ball.

2. Go to the Motion panel, and expand the Assign Controller rollout if it isn't already visible.

3. Select the Transform track on the hierarchy list.

4. Click the [?] Assign Controller button.

5. Choose Link Constraint from the list. The Link Constraint controller has now been assigned to the ball.

   First you'll need to link the ball to a stationary object in the scene. The chair is the only stationary object, so you'll link the ball to that object.

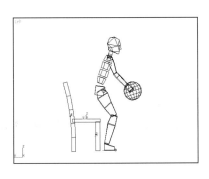

6. Go to frame 0.

7. On the Link Params rollout, click Add Link, and then click on any part of the chair.

   Next, you'll link the ball to the biped's hand at frame 50.

8. Go to frame 50.

9. Click on one of the biped's hands.

10. Click Add Link again to turn it off.

11. Play the animation.

    The biped stands up, bends over, picks up the ball, and then stands straight again. You'll find a finished version of this scene on the CD in the file `Pickup.max`.

Pinning the Hands to Objects

Suppose you want to create an animation with a biped standing in a moving subway car, holding onto an overhead handle. You'd want the biped's feet to stay on the floor and its hand to stay on the handle, while its body moves around with the motion of the subway. We could do this with techniques we've already seen in this chapter, but here we'll create this effect with Biped's Anchor tools. These tools let you temporarily fix the arms and legs in space. They're legacy functions from the earliest versions of the software—but don't discount them for being old; they still work.

The Anchor Left Arm and Anchor Right Arm buttons on the Keyframing Tools rollout can be used to anchor one or both hands in space without setting any particular linkage. (And of course there are Anchor Leg buttons for the lower limbs as well.) When you animate the rest of the body, the anchored hand will stay still. This is another tool that simplifies the IK mechanics for you.

Riding the Subway

In this exercise, you'll take the biped on a bumpy subway ride as it holds on to an overhead handle.

1. Load the file Subway.max from the CD.

   This file contains a biped with two standing footsteps lasting throughout the entire animation. It also contains a small torus to be used as a handle. The torus is frozen to make it easier for you to do the exercise.

2. Go to frame 0.

3. Turn on the Auto Key button.

4. Move the biped's right hand to the handle, and rotate the fingers around the handle.

   Check both the Front and Left viewports to make sure the hand and fingers are positioned properly.

5. Click ☝ Anchor Right Arm on the Keyframing Tools rollout. The hand is now anchored in space at its present location.

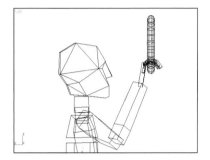

6. Go to frame 20.

7. On the Bend Links rollout, turn on ⌇ Twist Links mode.

8. Select the lowest spine link, and rotate the spine so that the biped bends to the left.

   With twist links on, all the spine objects rotate with the rotation of the selected link. You can also rotate the head a little bit, to go with the spine. Notice that the feet and the anchored hand stay still while the body bends.

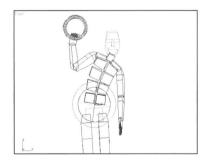

9. Click ↕ Body Vertical.

10. Move the COM downward to bend the knees.

11. Continue to move to other frames and animate any of the body parts. Notice that you can't move the feet because they are controlled by the footsteps, although you *can* rotate them as you like.

To make the biped's ride appear bumpy, you can rotate the spine, hips, or neck, or raise the free arm. You can also move the COM object downward to make the knees bend. Watch out—if you rotate the body too far, the hand will slip out of the ring even though it's anchored. (We'll learn how to fix this in the next section.)

A finished version of this animation can be found in the file `Bumpy_Ride.max` on the CD.

Making a Hand or Foot Follow Another Object

What if you want a biped's hand to follow an object? For example, suppose you want the biped to wash a window. Rather than animating the hand directly, it would be much easier to animate the sponge and link the hand to the sponge. However, you can't link the hand to the sponge because the hand is already linked to the arm—as it should be. To make a hand follow another object, you have to use a different method.

An *object-space object* (OSO) is an object that a hand or foot can follow through space instead of being constrained by the biped animation keys. The arm or leg animates according to the motion of the hand or foot that is following the object.

To get to the tools for selecting the object-space object, expand the IK section in the Key Info rollout.

You'll encounter the terms *world space* and *object space* in the Character Studio documentation from time to time. When no OSO is selected (and IK Blend is 1 and the Object option is selected), the object is in world space. When an OSO is selected, the object is in object space (hence the term *object-space object*).

►NOTE◄

If the OSO moves too far away from the body, the arm or leg goes completely straight and then detaches from the object. In other words, the body doesn't follow along automatically (although it can be animated to do so manually, if you wish).

To make a foot or hand follow an OSO, use the settings on the Key Info rollout. In order for the hand or foot to follow the object, IK Blend must be set to 1, and the Object option must be selected. In addition, you must click the Select IK Object button and then click the object that you want the hand or foot to follow. The name of the selected object then appears in the box to the left of the Select IK Object button.

Compare this process with your earlier uses of IK Blend and the Object setting. When no OSO was selected, having IK Blend set to 1 and Object selected caused the foot or hand to stay still—that's because Character Studio considered that the hand or foot was actually stuck to its current position in space. When an OSO is selected, with IK Blend set to 1 and Object selected, Character Studio considers that the hand or foot is stuck to the object, not to a spot in world space.

EXERCISE 9.3

Swingin' Biped

In this exercise, you'll animate a character on a backyard swing.

1. Load the file Swing.max from the CD.

   This file contains a child on a swing.

2. Select the named selection set Child Parts, and hide it. Then unhide the biped with the named selection set Biped. Once the biped is unhidden, clear the selection set or subsequent steps won't work cleanly.

3. Play the animation.

   The swing currently moves out from under the biped. Our job will be to make the biped move along with the swing.

4. Go to frame 0.

5. In the Left viewport, zoom in on the biped's hip area.

6. On the main toolbar, click Select and Link.

7. Link the COM to the swing seat.

8. Play the animation.

   The biped now moves with the seat. So far, so good.

Use OSO to Attach Hands

If we rotated the spine at this point to make the biped sway realistically, the biped's hands would become disengaged from the swing bars. So first we'll use an OSO on each hand to keep them attached to the bars.

1. Turn on Auto Key, then go to frame 0 and select any part of the left arm or hand.

2. On the Key Info rollout, expand the IK section.

3. Click ⬀ Select IK Object, and select the bar that the biped is holding with its left hand.

   To the left of the Select IK Object button, the object name `Swing bar left` appears. You've just designated the Swing object as the object for the hand to stick to.

4. Set IK Blend to 1 and choose the Object option. With this setting, the hand will now actually stick to the object.

5. Select any part of the right arm or hand.

6. On the Key Info rollout, click ⬀ Select IK Object. Select the bar that the biped is holding with its right hand.

7. Set IK Blend to 1 and choose the Object option.

   Now both hands will stick to the swing.

►NOTE◄

You have to select the OSO *before* setting IK Blend and Object. Choosing the OSO always resets IK Blend to 0 and enables the Body setting.

Rock the Biped

Now we want the biped to rock back and forth and pump its legs, the way a child does on a swing.

1. Go to frame 15.

2. Click ⟳ Body Rotation.

3. Make sure the Auto Key button is still on.

4. In the Left viewport, rotate the COM backward by about 25 degrees.

   The biped's hands stay attached to the swing bars.

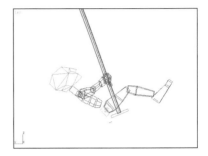

5. Rotate the lower legs so that they form roughly a 120 degree angle with the upper legs, as shown in the figure.

6. Rotate the head to look upward.

7. Go to frame 22.

8. Position the legs nearly straight against the seat.

9. Select the lowest spine link, and click ⊙ Set Key.

   Getting a key here will keep the lowest spine link in the right place when we animate it later.

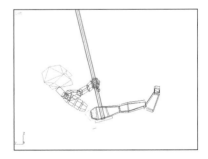

Pose the Backswing

Now we'll set up the backswing. For the highest point of the swing backward, we want to copy and paste the leg pose from frame 0.

1. Go to frame 0.

2. Select the COM, the head, and the biped's legs.

3. In the Copy/Paste field, click ▦ Create Collection; then click ▣ Copy Posture.

4. In the Copied Postures field, name the posture UPRIGHT.

5. Go to frame 45.

   This is the highest point of the backswing.

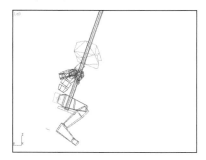

6. Click 📋 Paste Posture, then click the biped Set Key to keyframe the pasted posture.

7. In the Left viewport, rotate the lowest spine link forward by about 35 degrees, and rotate the COM to move the biped's legs toward the seat.

Loop and Finish the Animation

Now we'll copy and paste the posture at frame 0 to the last frame, to make a looping animation.

1. Go to frame 0.

2. Select the COM, the lowest spine link, and the biped's legs.

3. Click Copy Posture and name the copied posture START.

4. Go to frame 60.

5. Click Paste Posture. Now click Set Key.

6. Play the animation.

   The biped swings back and forth, pumping its legs to work up some momentum.

7. Hide the biped, and unhide the named selection set Child Parts.

8. Play the animation and watch the child swing back and forth.

   You'll find a finished version of this exercise in the file SwingAnim1.max on the CD. To see a rendered version, view the animation file Swing_anim.avi on the CD.

Animating OSO Settings

You can animate the IK Blend and Body/Object settings to make a hand or foot follow another object at some times, and not follow it at other times. You set the IK Blend to 0 and the Body/Object setting to Body to make the hand or foot stop following the object; then you animate IK Blend back to 1 and choose Object to make the hand or foot again follow the object.

EXERCISE 9.4

Pushing the Swing

In this exercise, you'll animate the OSO to make a mother push a child on a swing. Here, the child's lowest spine link will become the OSO for the mother's hands. As the child swings back to the mother, her hands will follow the child's body and appear to push him.

1. Load the file PushSwing.max from the CD and play the animation.

   This scene includes the child on the swing from the preceding exercise. His mother has come to push the swing for him. Right now, the OSO has not been set up, so the child passes right through the mother's hands.

2. Go to frame 40.

   This is the frame where the child's body reaches the mother's hands.

3. In the Left viewport, zoom in on the child's lowest spine link.

4. Select the mother's left hand.

5. In the Key Info rollout's IK section, click [⤢] Select IK Object, and click the child's lowest spine link.

   The object name Child Spine should appear next to the Select IK Object button.

6. Set IK Blend to 1 and choose the Object option.

7. Select the mother's right hand, and set up the OSO in the same way. Make sure to zoom in sufficiently in the viewport so that you can click on the correct object.

8. Play the animation.

   The mother's hands come up and then start to follow the child's body at frame 40. After the child swings away from the mother around frame 50, the mother continues to stretch out her hands.

Set More OSO Keys

Before you set up the OSO for the hands, keys for the hands were already set at frames 0 and 30. At those frames, IK Blend is 0 and Body is selected. The OSO doesn't kick in until frame 40. However, it lasts through to the end of the animation, which we don't want to happen.

1. Go to frame 51.

    This is the last frame in which we want the mother's hands to follow the child's body. Here, we'll set a key for the OSO.

2. Select the mother's left hand, and click Set Key.

    Because IK Blend is currently 1 and Object is selected, a key is set with these values.

3. Select the mother's right hand, and click Set Key.

4. Go to frame 60.

5. With the hand still selected, click Set Key.

6. Change IK Blend to 0 and choose Body.

    This will cause the hand to stop following the body after frame 51. Now we can set keys for the arm and hand at frame 60 to position them wherever we like. Of course, none of this affects the child's keys.

7. Select the mother's left hand, and click Set Key.

8. Change IK Blend to 0 and choose Body.

Copy Arm Positions

Now we can copy and paste the arm positions from frame 0 to frame 60 to create a looping animation.

1. Go to frame 0.

2. Select both of the mother's arms, including the hands.

3. On the Copy/Paste rollout, click Create Collection and then Copy Posture.

4. Go to frame 60.

5. Turn on the Auto Key button.

6. Click Paste Posture.

   The mother's arms now relax on frame 60.

7. Play the animation.

   The mother pushes her child on the swing, releasing the child at frame 51.

Loosen Up, Mom

Our work with the OSO is complete. However, the animation of the mother is a little stiff. Let's add some life to her.

1. Go to frame 0.

2. Click Body Horizontal for the mother biped.

3. Make sure Auto Key is on.

4. In the Left viewport, move the COM to the left by about 80 units.

5. Go to frame 25.

6. Click Set Key.

7. Go to frame 40.

8. In the Left viewport, move the COM to the right until the mother's head nearly touches the child's head.

   Because the OSO is in effect on this frame, the mother's arms will bend as she is moved closer to the child.

9. Go to frame 60.

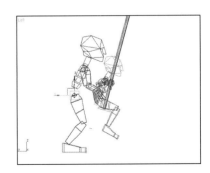

10. Move the COM to the left so that the mother sways back away from the child.

Now the mother moves back and forth as she pushes the child.

You can do additional work on this scene if you like, to make the arms' motion less abrupt. You can also animate the mother's head and neck so that she looks at the child or looks away during the animation. You'll find a finished version of this scene in the file `PushSwing_Anim.max` on the CD.

Bulges

Bulges can be used to make parts of the mesh bulge out when a certain angle is achieved between two consecutive links. For example, when a character flexes its arm, a bulge can appear in the bicep.

Bulges don't work with ordinary keys; they work with angles. When the angle between one joint and the next is achieved, the bulge appears.

You set up bulges as an option under either the Physique or Skin modifier. In the Physique modifier, the Bulge sub-object is used to set the angle for the bulge, and the amount by which the mesh bulges when the angle is achieved. In the Skin modifier, you can select vertices and add a Bulge Angle Deformer gizmo to accomplish the same thing. You can find detailed information about these in the 3ds Max User Reference.

EXERCISE 9.5

Workout Woman

The easiest way to show how bulges are set up is to do an exercise with them. Bulges are computationally intensive, so it's best to experiment with them on a low-polygon model.

1. Load the file `She_workout.max` from the CD and play the animation.

This file contains a low-polygon model of a woman in a workout suit. She's been exercising a lot lately and wants to show you her muscles. The woman lifts her arm and flexes it. There's no bulging muscle there yet, but there will be soon.

2. Go to frame 70.

   This is where the flex is at its maximum. This is the angle at which we want the muscle bulge to appear.

3. In the User viewport, zoom in on the woman's flexed arm.

4. Select the mesh. The mesh is all one object, so you can select it by clicking any part of it.

5. Go to the Modify panel.

6. Expand the Physique modifier, and choose Bulge as the sub-object level.

7. Click on the upper arm in the User viewport. Don't worry that you can't see the bones.

   A green lattice appears around the upper and lower arms, indicating that the bulge will be set for the upper arm based on its angle with the lower arm. The lattice has a yellow line projecting from the armpit, which you can see if you rotate around the mesh in the User viewport.

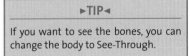

►TIP◄

If you want to see the bones, you can change the body to See-Through.

8. In the Cross Section Parameters section of the Bulge rollout, change Sections to 4.

   As you change the number of sections, you'll see more green cross-sections appear on the upper arm lattice.

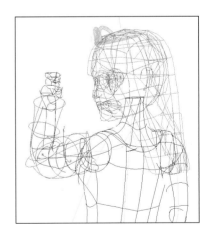

9. At the top of the Bulge rollout, click ⊡ Bulge Editor.

The Bulge Editor window appears.

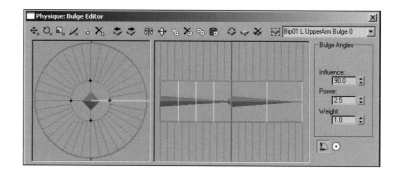

Edit the Bulge

The Bulge Editor window has two sections. The horizontal bar on the right represents a side view of the upper and lower arms. The vertical bars are sections dividing the arm. Notice that the vertical bars to the left of the red line divide the area into four sections, representing the four cross-sections of the upper arm.

The circular display at the left is a cross-section view as if you are looking down the arm. Notice that one side has a yellow line going through it. This corresponds to the yellow line going up the back of the arm along the bulge lattice.

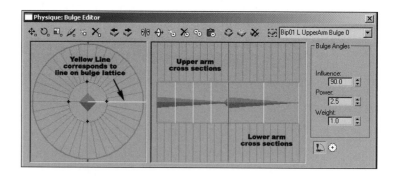

1. Click ⊡ Insert Bulge Angle.

This starts a new bulge angle key for the upper arm.

2. Click on the center vertical section bar for the upper arm, as shown in the figure.

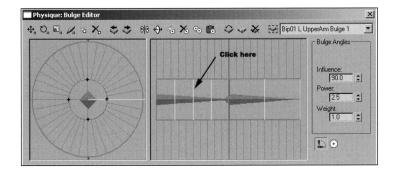

3. In the Bulge Editor window, click the ⊕ Select, Scale, Rotate Ctrl Pts button.

4. On the circular display at the left of the Bulge Editor window, move the topmost point upward, about halfway to the outside circle.

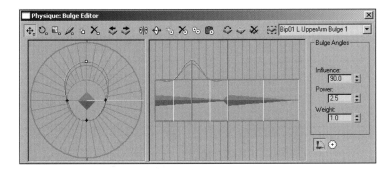

As you move the point, you'll see a muscle bulge appear on the woman's arm.

5. In the Bulge Editor, click on the vertical section bar to the right of the currently selected section.

6. Move the topmost point of the circular display upward, about a quarter of the way to the outer circle.

What we're going for here is a smooth muscle bulge.

7. Continue to work with the upper-arm vertical sections and the circular display until the bulge looks good in the viewport.

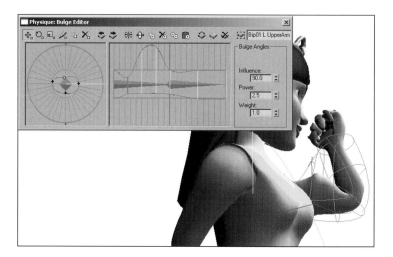

8. When the muscle bulge looks good, click ⬡ Set Bulge Angle to set the angle key.

9. Close the Bulge Editor.

10. Click Physique at the top of the stack to turn off Sub-Object on the Modify panel.

11. Play the animation.

   Each time the woman straightens her arm, the bulge disappears. When she flexes her arm, a big muscle appears. You don't want to mess with this woman! You'll find a finished version of this scene in the file She_workout_bulge.max on the CD.

Combining Motions

One of Character Studio's finest features is its ability to utilize motions in a variety of ways. You can combine the motions of several bipeds on one biped, or repeat the motions of one biped on several bipeds.

You can also use a sequence of motions on several bipeds or other characters. You can choose the order of motions yourself, or you can have Character Studio make choices about which motions to use when. This feature is particularly useful for crowd scenes, where you want characters to use all the same motions but at different times. The choice of motions can be designed to make the characters move toward a goal or to keep them from bumping into one another, just as characters behave in real life.

The heart of all these techniques is the collection of motions you create and save individually. In this section, you'll learn how to create motions and combine them using a number of tools.

CHAPTER 10

Motion Mixer and Motion Flow

Each animation (*motion*) you create can be saved as a separate file with the extension .BIP. These motion files can be mixed and matched on other bipeds.

The ability to load and save motions lets you switch among different rigs or skeletons and apply the same animations to all of them, or load the actions of one character onto another. Once you've loaded a BIP file onto a biped, you can adjust the animation with any of Character Studio's tools. You can also append one motion to another, and combine motions to create completely new animated sequences.

Character Studio includes two powerful methods for combining motions: the Motion Mixer and the Motion Flow tools.

Comparing Motion Mixer and Motion Flow

The *Motion Mixer* allows you to separate and combine pieces of motion (animation) and mix them together as you like. Similar to a video editing program, the Mixer is a single, powerful tool for nonlinear editing of animation files.

Motion Flow comprises a set of tools for combining motions. With Motion Flow, you place BIP files on a graph and link them via transitions from one motion to another.

In 3ds Max 5 and prior versions, Motion Flow was the only method available for combining motions. The Motion Mixer was introduced as a quicker, easier method for straight motion sequencing with transitions. The Motion Mixer also contributes several new features, such as the ability to use different motions on various biped parts. However, Motion Flow is still necessary for creating random sequences and for setting up biped crowd scenes.

Feature	Motion Mixer	Motion Flow
Can perform motions in sequence, with intelligent transitions in between	X	X
Allows the use of particular motions on different body parts (such as one motion for arms, another for legs)	X	–
Includes special effects such as slowing down or speeding up motions	X	–
Can create a single BIP motion file from the combined motions	X	–
Can create a network of BIP files for use with biped crowd scenes	–	X
Can generate random motion sequences from a set of BIP files	–	X

Motion Files

At the heart of both the Motion Mixer and Motion Flow tools are motion files, saved with a .bip extension. A BIP file, also called a clip, is different from a MAX file. In a BIP file, only the motions are saved, indepedent of the biped. You can use BIP files to build up libraries of motions, which you can then load and combine with other motions on any biped.

To create a BIP file, first you animate the biped with any method, including footsteps or freeform in Character Studio, motion capture of a live actor, or even animation in another program. How you save the motion as a BIP file depends on your animation method:

- In Character Studio, save the completed motion by selecting the biped and clicking [icon] Save File on the Biped rollout of the Motion panel.

- For motion capture, load the motions onto a biped and use Save File for each motion.

- In other character animation packages, check the documentation to find out how to save motions.

To load a BIP file on a biped, select any part of the biped. On the Biped rollout of the Motion panel, click [icon] Load File and choose the BIP file.

►NOTE◄

Now in 3ds Max 8, you can also save the animation from a bones rig as an XAF file, the new native file format for animation. This provides the same functionality for Max objects as the BIP file does for biped skeletons.

EXERCISE 10.1

Working with Motions

In this exercise, you'll load a sample BIP file onto a biped. Then you'll create an animation and save it as motion files of your own.

Load a Motion

1. Create a biped of any size. With the biped selected, go to the Motion panel, and on the Biped rollout click [icon] Load File.

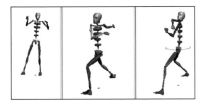

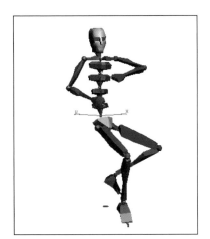

2. Navigate to the \Samples\Motion\BIP_RedEyeStudio\ Swords_Ax folder on the 3ds Max 8 installation DVD, and open the file boswipe.bip.

   The animation in that BIP file is now loaded on your biped.

3. Play the animation in any viewport. If the biped disappears from the viewport, zoom and pan as needed to get a new view; then play the animation again.

   The biped now performs a kind of martial-arts move, whirling its hands around its head, perhaps like stick-fighting.

4. Now load the file boswipe_kick.bip. With the biped selected, go to the Motion panel. On the Biped rollout, click [icon] Load File and then select the file boswipe_kick.bip.

   The new motion loads, and the previous one is gone.

5. Play the animation. In this one, the biped is again doing the stick-fighting motion, but then it spins and kicks at around frame 92.

6. Now go to \Samples\Motion\BIP\Eat_Drink on the 3ds Max DVD and load BarStoolSit.bip and play this animation. A biped walks into a bar and sits on an invisible bar stool.

7. Load the file BarStoolStnd.bip from the same directory as the previous BIP file and play this animation. The biped gets up off the stool, waves goodbye, and walks away.

Save a Motion

Saving a motion file is almost as easy as loading a BIP file. Just animate with any method (we'll use footsteps here) and then save.

1. Create a biped of any size.

2. Create an eight-footstep motion, and click [icon] Create Keys for Inactive Footsteps to activate the footsteps.

3. Test the animation by clicking Play. The biped walks through the eight footsteps.

4. With the biped selected, click 🖫 Save File on the Biped roll-out. Save the motion file with the name WALKSTEPS.BIP.

   This is different from saving a MAX file. Here, only the selected biped's motion is saved.

5. Reset 3ds Max, and create a new biped of any size.

6. With the biped selected, click 📂 Load File on the Biped rollout of the Motion panel. Load the file you just created, WALKSTEPS.BIP.

   The same footstep animation you just saved is loaded onto the biped.

7. Click Play to watch the biped go through the same motions.

Motion Mixer

In addition to simply loading motion files onto other bipeds, you can use the Motion Mixer to segment motions and then piece them together differently.

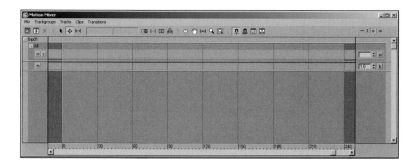

The Motion Mixer works with tracks, similar to those you've seen in Track View. The Motion Mixer's tracks hold whole BIP files, rather than individual transforms. You can set up numerous tracks for an individual biped and put BIP files on each track. The clip's position on the track determines when in the animation the biped will perform that motion.

When you open the Motion Mixer, by clicking the Mixer button on the Biped Apps rollout, you'll see a track for each biped in the scene. The tracks are labeled with the name of the biped.

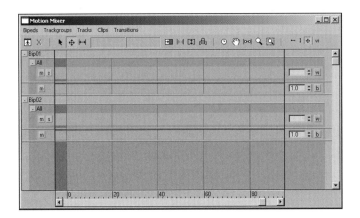

There are three types of tracks in the Motion Mixer:

- A *layer track* consists of a single slot. BIP files can be placed on this type of track sequentially only, with no overlap or transitions between the clips.

Layer track

- A *transition track* consists of three slots. The upper and lower slots are for BIP files, and the middle slot holds a transition between the two BIP files.

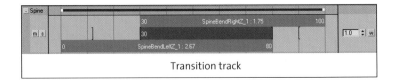

Transition track

- The *balance track* is the smaller track sitting below each biped's other tracks. This track is used to calculate the biped's balance (more on this later in this chapter).

Opening the Motion Mixer automatically enables the ⬚ Mixer Mode button on the Biped rollout. When Mixer Mode is on, the biped follows the motion indicated by the Motion Mixer setup. When Mixer Mode is off, the biped follows the animation you have set up in the scene with Biped tools. (Later in this chapter, we'll perform what's called a mixdown, so that the biped always performs the Motion Mixer animation. This makes it possible to save a BIP file of the animation.)

The Motion Mixer automatically inserts a transition between two clips in a transition track. However, you'll want to optimize it to achieve the smoothest transition between two clips. *Optimization* is an automatic process that looks for logical transition points, such as places where the feet match up. When no close matches are found, optimization does its best to make a smooth transition. If you're careful in choosing or setting up the BIP files used in the Motion Flow Graph, optimization is usually very successful.

To start the optimization process, right-click a transition clip and choose Optimize. The Transition Optimization dialog appears. Here you can choose whether to limit the transition to selected frames, or to search entire clips for the best transitions. If you're using long clips and have already worked with the transition to get it near the place where you want it, choose Search Near Existing Transition. If you're using short clips, Search Entire Clip is the best option. Then click OK to start the process, and wait a few moments while the transitions are optimized.

EXERCISE 10.2

Working with the Motion Mixer

In this exercise, we'll combine two clips in the Motion Mixer. Then we'll add a transition track to create a transition between the two clips.

1. Reset 3ds Max.

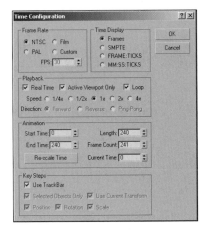

2. Click Time Configuration below the Viewport playback controls at the bottom-right of the 3ds Max interface, and set Length to 240. Click OK to close the dialog.

   Now the animation is long enough for the two clips and the transition.

3. Create a new biped of any size.

4. With the biped still selected, go to the Motion panel and click Mixer in the Biped Apps rollout.

   The Motion Mixer window appears, showing the default of one track for the currently selected biped.

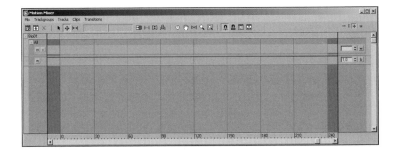

5. Right-click a blank area of the track. From the pop-up menu that appears, choose Convert to Transition Track.

   This makes the track space taller. Now you can place one motion file on the bottom of the track, another on the top, and have a transition between them.

6. Right-click the track again and choose New Clips > From Files > boswipe.bip.

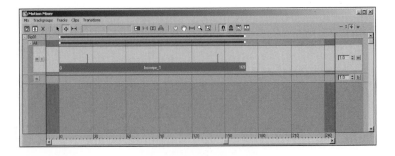

This clip is added to the Motion Mixer. If you play the animation in the viewport, the biped runs through the stick-fighter movement from the preceding exercise.

7. Right-click again on the track. Choose New Clips > From Files > `boswipe_kick.bip`.

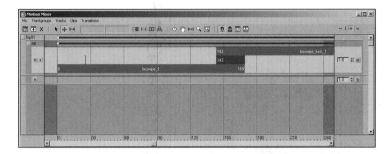

Now a second motion file is added to the mix. A short transition time appears between the two motions.

8. In the Motion Mixer toolbar, click ⊙ Set Range.

This extends the active time segment in 3ds Max to be long enough for both animations.

9. In the Motion Mixer toolbar, click |o-o| Zoom Extents.

If you play the animation now, you'll see first `boswipe.bip` and then `boswipe_kick.bip` play in sequence, with a 26-frame transition starting at frame 143.

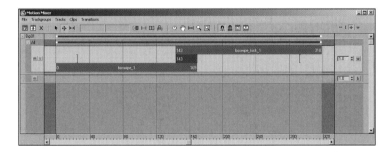

Optimize Transitions

Watch carefully, and you'll notice that the transition between the two motions (`boswipe.bip` and `boswipe_kick.bip`) is far from

perfect. During frames 143 through 169, both of the biped's feet ice-skate across the floor. You can try for a better transition by using the Optimize command.

1. On the Edit menu choose Hold. Right-click the transition between the clips, and choose Optimize to open the Transition Optimization dialog.

2. Accept all the defaults in the dialog and click OK.

   The transition is now positioned at frame 115 and is only 10 frames long.

3. Play the animation. The transition is less noticeable and takes place at a better point between the actions.

Edit Transition

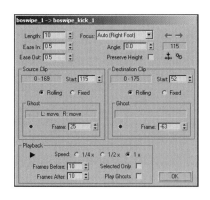

If you don't like the transition that Transition Optimization has found, you can edit it to get it exactly the way you like.

1. On the Edit menu choose Fetch. If the Mixer disappears, restart the Mixer. Right-click the transition and choose Edit.

2. In the transition editor, you can set the exact length and start frame of the transition.

3. In the Playback section turn on Play Ghosts. Click the ▶ Play Transition button in the Playback section to see a viewport display of the destination clip as a red stick-figure, and the source clip as a yellow stick-figure.

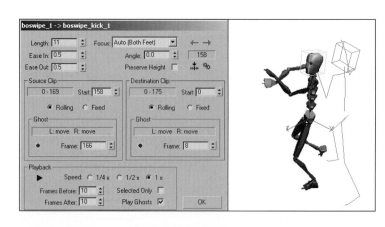

If you don't see the stick figures when you playback, try scrubbing the time-slider. Depending on your video card you may experience a bug that doesn't show the stick figures during playback.

4. Try to find a place where the red and yellow stick-figures are close to each other, and use that as the start of the transition. In this example, if you set the transition to be about 11 frames long between frames 158 and 169, you'll have less noticeable foot sliding.

►TIP◄

Use the Angle setting in the transition editor to orient the direction of the second clip. Enter various values into the Angle field and watch the update in the viewport.

Weighting Tracks

You can stack up a series of tracks and *weight* each one, so that several clips affect a biped to varying degrees. The weight determines how much a clip or transition affects the biped.

To create a stack of tracks, right-click any track and choose one of the Add options from the pop-up menu. Although it's possible to create a stack of up to 99 tracks, two or three tracks are usually enough.

By default, a track has a weight of 1 throughout the animation, but weights can vary from 0 to 1. On a transition track, the weight value applies to the entire track, transition and all. A weight of 1 indicates that a track affects the biped by 100 percent, and the total weight of all tracks always adds up to 1, calculated from the top of the stack down. That means when you lower the weight of the top track to be less than 1, the tracks below the top track affect the biped motion by a correspondingly higher percentage.

For example, if the clip on the topmost track has a weight of 0.3 at a particular frame, it affects the biped by 30 percent, and the next track down is evaluated. If the clip on the second track has a weight of 0.7 or more, it affects the biped by 70 percent, and any tracks below the second track are not evaluated. But if the second track's weight is less than 0.7, the next track down is evaluated until the total weight adds up to 1.

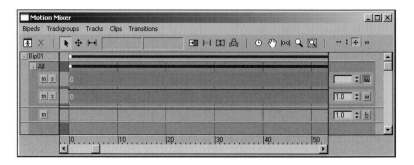

You can enable changes to a track's weight by clicking the w button to the right of the track. This w and the line across the top of the track both turn red, and you can select one of the default points at the start or end of the clip. Or you can click anywhere on the red line to create a new point. Then change the weight by dragging the point up or down or by changing the value of the spinner next to the w button.

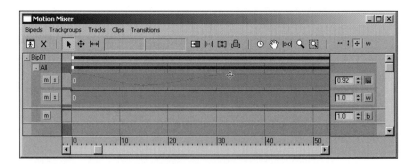

After you've finished working with weights, be sure to turn off the w button so that you can move clips and work with them in the Motion Mixer.

Working with Trackgroups

You can also use the Motion Mixer to take the upper body movement from one BIP file and the lower body movement from another. This is accomplished with the use of *trackgroups*.

A trackgroup is a group of tracks that affect one set of body parts. For example, you could have one set of tracks that affect the arms, another for the legs, and yet another for the head. The tracks in a trackgroup can be layer tracks, transition tracks, or a combination of the two.

EXERCISE 10.3

Mixing Upper and Lower Body Motions

1. Reset 3ds Max and create a new biped.

2. Click Mixer on the Motion panel to open the Motion Mixer. Right-click the default layer track and choose New Clips > From Files > GunFighter.bip.

3. Click [icon] Set Range and [icon] Zoom Extents.

   This ensures that there are enough frames in the 3ds Max time configuration to accommodate the clip you loaded into the Motion Mixer.

4. Arc-rotate your viewport in order to see the animation. Play the animation. The biped takes five steps, then draws and shoots an invisible gun.

5. Right-click the label marked All just below the Bip01, and from the pop-up menu choose Add Trackgroup Below.

> **►NOTE◄**
> The Biped layers you used in Chapter 8, "Body Animation," were a first stab at the kind of functionality achieved through trackgroups. With basic Biped layers, you can only add a layer to the existing motion, but not actually load files into that layer—you have to animate by hand once you've created the layer. Layers in Motion Mixer, however, let you add multiple clips one after another.

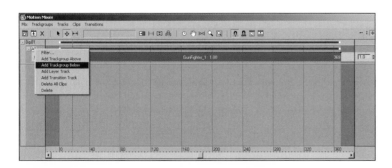

6. Click in the new trackgroup; then right-click and choose Convert to Transition Track. Right-click again and choose Convert to Layer Track. (This is a workaround to make sure that the next steps work correctly.)

7. Right-click in the track, and choose New Clips > From Files > `Hambone.bip`.

Filter Tracks

If you play the animation now, you won't see anything different from before, because `GunFighter.bip` is taking precedence over the `hambone.bip` animation. Next, you will filter these two tracks.

1. Right-click the label marked All in the first trackgroup (`GunFighter.bip`) and choose Filter.

2. In the Trackgroup Filter dialog, click the upper body parts to deselect them and then click OK.

    This filters out the animation in the upper body, so that the gunfighter motions will not be applied to these trackgroups.

3. Right-click the label marked All in the *second* trackgroup (`hambone.bip`), and choose Filter.

4. Click the lower body parts to deselect them, and then click OK.

5. Play the animation.

    The biped performs the upper-body motion from the `hambone.bip` file and the lower-body motion from the `GunFighter.bip` animation. He approaches like a gunfighter, except that his upper body is doing the hambone. It looks like as though he's trying to fake out the other gunslinger, which is perhaps not the smartest thing to do.

6. Save the scene as `Fakeout.max`.

The Balance Track

When you mix upper- and lower-body motions, the biped's hips can react unrealistically. For example, if the upper body is thrown forward, the biped's hips might not compensate adequately if the COM uses a different clip for its motion.

The balance track, the lowest track in the Motion Mixer for each biped, can adjust the biped's balance to make it more realistic. It works with a system similar to track weighting. When you turn on the b button at the right end of the track, you can adjust the balance value between 0 and 1 to shift the biped's weight forward or back.

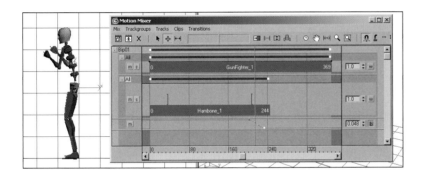

Mixdowns

Remember, the animation in the Motion Mixer affects the biped only if Mixer mode is turned on (the default state when Motion Mixer is opened). However, you can "glue" the Motion Mixer animation to the biped so that it affects the biped even when you exit Mixer mode. You do this by performing a *mixdown* on the animation and applying it to the biped.

A mixdown takes all the motion in the Motion Mixer and turns it into a single animation file that you can apply to the biped. After the file is applied to the biped, you can exit the Motion Mixer and turn off Mixer mode, and the biped will still perform the motions. In addition, you can then save the entire motion as a BIP file in the usual way.

EXERCISE 10.4

Performing a Mixdown

1. Continue with your scene from the preceding exercise, or load the file Fakeout.max. Select the biped, and click Mixer on the Motion panel to open the Motion Mixer.

2. In the Motion Mixer, select the Bipo1 label at the top of the mixer tracks.

3. From the Mix menu at the top of the Motion Mixer window, choose Compute Mixdown. On the Mixdown Options dialog click OK.

The motions are computed into a mixdown track that appears below the other trackgroups.

Of course, if you change the Mixdown Options values, you'll have to compute the mixdown again. Undo the previous mixdown and try again with the new values.

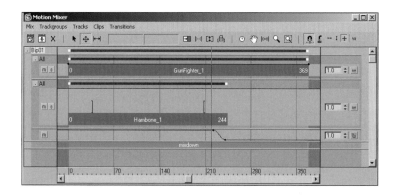

The Mixdown Options dialog gives you settings for the Maximum Knee Angle allowed. Mixdown Options also let you generate a keyframe per frame. If you're using motion capture, keep this turned on to maintain the level of detail in your action.

4. Play the animation and see if you like it.

   The mixdown track attempts to correct transitions between planted keys, and also tries to fix any hyperextensions of the leg.

5. Access the default mixdown settings by clicking the ▣ Preferences button in the Motion Mixer toolbar.

6. Once the final mixdown is computed, choose Mix > Copy Mixdown to Biped.

   The biped in the viewport now has the animation tracks from the mixdown. Even if you turn off 🐾 Mixer Mode, the biped will still perform this animation, which can then be saved to a BIP file.

7. Close the Motion Mixer.

8. On the Biped menu, turn off Mixer mode.

9. Play the animation.

   Though Mixer mode is off, the animation from the Motion Mixer still plays on the biped.

10. On the Biped menu, click 💾 Save File, and save the motion as FAKEOUT.BIP.

Time Warps

In the Motion Mixer, you can change the time within a clip to make it occupy a longer or shorter time in the scene. To stretch or shorten the time in a clip, right-click a clip on a track and choose Add Time Warp. If you then edit the time warp, the appearance of the clip will change to show a series of lines, which you can alter to adjust the clip's time.

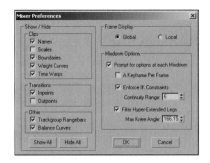

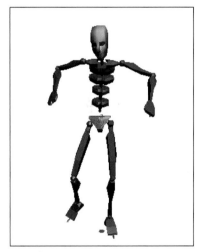

▶TIP◀

The entire Motion Mixer Graph arrangement of clips, transitions, and weighting for an individual biped can be saved as a MIX file, which you can then load into the Motion Mixer for any biped. To save a MIX file, choose Save Mix File from the Mix menu within the Motion Mixer.

EXERCISE 10.5

Adding a Time Warp

1. Reset 3ds Max and create a new biped.

2. Click Mixer on the Motion panel's Biped Apps rollout, to open the Motion Mixer dialog.

3. Right-click the Bip01 track and choose New Clips > From Files, and load `\Samples\Motion\BIP\Gymnastics\BroadJump.bip`.

4. Click ⏰ Set Ranges and |o-o| Zoom Extents.

5. Play the animation using the time slider. Notice that the jumper is airborne between frames 117 and 134.

6. Right-click the clip and choose Add Time Warp.

7. On the Motion Mixer toolbar, click |⊷| Editable Time Warps.

   A dotted horizontal line divides the track in two.

8. On the Motion Mixer toolbar, click the Select icon. Move your cursor over the time warp and click near frame 117. Click again near frame 134.

9. Use the Motion Mixer's 🔍 Zoom Region button to zoom in to the time warp.

   Although it looks like there are two range lines in the time warp, actually there are four lines. You can select and move the upper half of each of these lines to dictate the time warp. The lower range represents the frames to be warped, and the upper range of lines defines the time into which the clip will be stretched to fit.

   Here, the range of frames from 117 to 134 has been stretched to cover frames 111 to 143.

10. Play the animation in the viewport.

The airborne period now has a slow-motion effect added by the time warp. To see a file with this effect in place, load `slowjump.max`.

Motion Flow

Motion flow is an animation technique that uses two or more motion files in sequence to produce one animation. Character Studio's Motion Flow feature takes short motion sequences and creates transitions between them to create a longer sequence, or *script*. With the Motion Flow tools, you can control when each transition takes place, and how long it lasts.

You can create two types of motion flow: *straight-ahead* or *random*. With straight-ahead motion flow, you set up the clips in the script in the exact order you would like them to occur. With random motion flow, you set up multiple transitions, and the random script generator creates a script by choosing transitions at random. Random script generation is particularly useful for generating different scripts for several bipeds at the same time (more on this in Chapter 13).

Note that you can produce many of the same motion-flow results using the Motion Mixer.

In order to use the Motion Flow tools, you must set up the clips and transitions in the Motion Flow Graph, which is the control center for your clips and transitions.

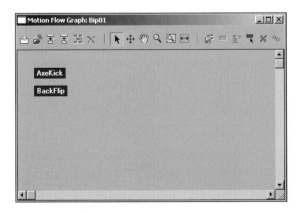

Creating Transitions

On a Motion Flow Graph, a transition is represented by an arrow going between two clips on the graph. You must create the transitions manually, but you can do so in a number of ways:

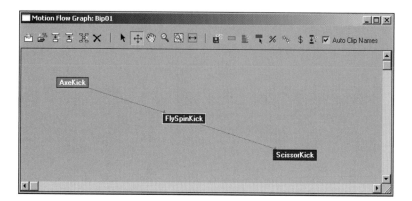

- Click 🔲 Define Script on the Motion Flow rollout, and click each clip you want to use on the Motion Flow Graph, in sequence. Transitions are automatically created between consecutive clips, and the new script is listed in the Motion Flow Script rollout.

- Click the 🔲 Create Transition To button on the Motion Flow Graph, and click and drag between clips. You can also click a clip to create a transition to itself.

- Click 🔲 Create All Transitions on the Motion Flow Graph to create all possible transitions between clips. This feature is useful when preparing to generate random scripts.

By default, each transition is created with a length of 25 frames, taking place over the last 25 frames of one clip and the first 25 frames of the next. Usually, you'll want to edit the default transitions to make them work with your clips.

Transitions can be adjusted manually, but it's best to optimize them first to see if workable transitions have been created. Optimizing transitions in Motion Flow is very similar to optimizing transitions in the Motion Mixer.

To optimize transitions in Motion Flow, first select the transitions on the graph, by clicking Select Clip/Transition on the Motion Flow Graph. Draw a bounding area around all transitions to select them. You can also select individual transitions by holding down the Ctrl key and clicking on each one. When a transition is selected, the transition line turns white.

Next, click Optimize Selected Transitions on the Motion Flow Graph. When the Transition Optimization dialog appears, select your options and click OK to start the optimization process. Wait a few moments while transitions are optimized.

A *transition cost* is a value assigned to each transition when it is optimized. Transition costs are calculated based on the degree of motion loss and other factors. The lower the number, the better the transition. To see transition costs, click $ Show Optimal Transition Costs.

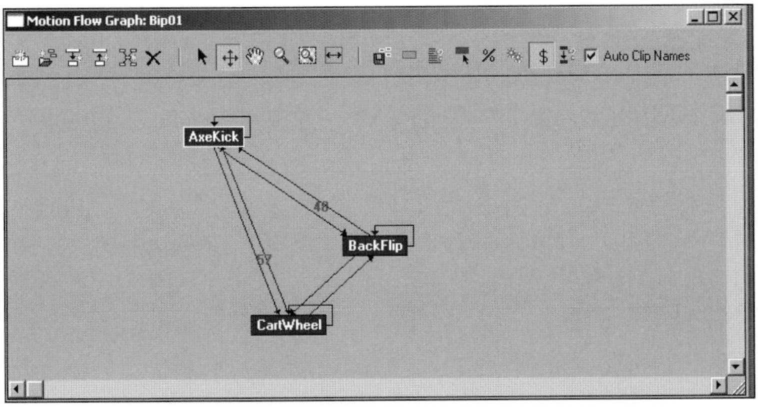

If the selected clips have logical transition points (such as times when both feet are down and a similar distance apart), the cost for the transition between them should not exceed 30. A very high transition cost, such as 200, indicates that the transition has significant motion loss and should probably be adjusted manually.

►NOTE◄

Manual changes to a transition will not affect the displayed transition cost. This number is generated only when transitions are optimized, and is intended to tell you about the optimized transition only.

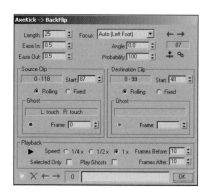

Manual transition editing is performed in the transition editor dialog, and there are two ways to open it and begin editing transitions:

- Right-click the transition line in the Motion Flow Graph.

- Highlight the clip in the script on the Motion Flow Script rollout, and click [icon] Edit Transition. This option is available only if you have clicked [icon] Define Script on the Motion Flow Script rollout and then selected two or more clips to define the script. If these transition editing tools seem familiar, they should—they are identical to the ones available for Motion Mixer transition editing.

In the transition editor, you can set the starting frames on each clip, and the length of the transition. You can also store more than one version of the same transition and choose the one you want to use. If you used the Define Script/Edit Transition method, you can use skeleton ghosts to help determine the best place for the transition.

Creating Straight-Ahead Motion Flow

In this exercise, you'll create a Motion Flow script with two clips. Then you'll use the transition editor to find the best transition.

1. Load the file BOY.MAX from the CD.

2. Unhide the named selection set Biped and hide the named selection set Child Parts.

   You are left with a child-sized biped.

3. Select any part of the biped, and click [icon] Motion Flow Mode in the Motion panel.

4. On the Motion Flow rollout, click [icon] Show Graph.

   The Motion Flow Graph appears.

5. In the graph window, click [icon] Create Multiple Clips.

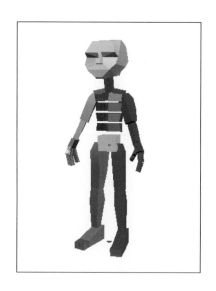

6. Navigate to the \Samples\Biped\Bip\kicks folder, and choose the file AxeKick.bip. Click Create Multiple Clips again, then navigate to the \gymnastics folder and choose BACKFLIP.BIP.

The two clips appear on the Motion Flow Graph.

Create and Optimize Transitions

Now that we have some clips in our script, we can add a transition between them.

1. Click [icon] Define Script on the Motion Flow rollout's Scripts area.

2. Click the AxeKick clip on the graph, and then click the Back-Flip clip.

An arrow appears on the graph, pointing from the first clip to the second, indicating that there is a transition between the two. The two motions also appear on the Motion Flow rollout.

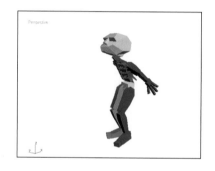

3. Click ⊞ Zoom Extents All to find the biped.

   Because we used the Define Script method, the biped is in the world space location where the BIP file was created. This means you'll have to change your views to find the biped.

4. Play the animation.

   You can see that there is a point around frame 95 where the biped drifts into the air. This is where the transition is taking place, and it reveals that the default transition is not working out very well for these two clips. There is also a point at frame 98 where the biped flips about 230 degrees in one frame.

5. Click ↖ Select Clip/Transition.

6. Click the transition to select it.

7. Click 🔧 Optimize Selected Transitions.

8. In the Transition Optimization dialog, choose Search Entire Clip, and enter 25 as the Preferred Transition Length. Click OK.

9. Play the animation.

   The biped now prepares for the flip with both feet on the ground. This is a much more natural transition.

Edit Transition

Let's take a closer look at the transition and see if we can get a better result manually. We'll use the transition editor's "ghost" feature to find a better transition. Then we'll compare the two transitions.

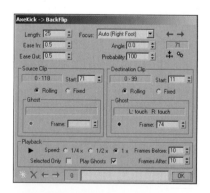

1. Highlight AxeKick on the Motion Flow rollout's Scripts area.

   The ⬚ Edit Transition button on the Motion Flow rollout's Scripts area is now available.

2. Click ⬚ Edit Transition.

   The transition editor appears. You can see that the first clip, the Source Clip, is set to start transitioning at frame 71. The transition has a Length of 25 frames.

3. In the Playback area of the transition editor, check the Play Ghosts check box, and then click the ▶ Play Transition button to play the animation.

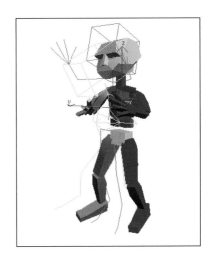

The biped has a yellow skeleton ghost through it at the beginning of the animation. At frame 71, a red skeleton ghost appears. The yellow skeleton shows the motion of the first clip, while the red skeleton shows the second clip. As you scrub through the animation, the biped gradually assumes more of the pose of the red skeleton. At frame 96, which is 25 frames after frame 71, the yellow skeleton disappears and the biped completely follows the red skeleton.

4. Locate the Ghost section under Source Clip on the transition editor.

5. Use the Frame spinner in the Ghost section to make the red ghost scrub through its motion.

Around frame 94, the yellow ghost's feet come together. This would also be a good spot for the biped's feet to land just before making the flip. We estimate that we want this to take place around the middle of the transition. The transition is 25 frames long, so starting the transition 12 frames earlier at frame 82 would probably work fine.

6. In the transition editor, click ▦ Create Transition at the lower-left corner of the dialog.

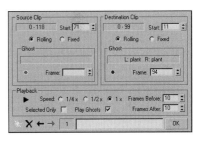

The number to the right of the Create Transition button has changed from 0 to 1. This indicates that we have stored the old transition while trying the new one. We're now editing transition number 1.

7. Under Source Clip, change the Start frame to 82.

8. Play or scrub through the animation.

This transition works just as well as the other one. You can simply choose the one that works best for your project. If you decide to use a different transition later, you can return to

Motion Flow mode, open the transition editor in the same way, and select the other transition.

9. To scroll through transitions, click ← Previous Transition and → Next Transition.

10. Click OK to close the transition editor.

    The transition that is active when you close the dialog is the one that is used in the script.

11. Hide the biped, and unhide the selection set Child Parts.

12. Play the animation.

    A final version of this exercise can be seen in the file BOY_MOTION.MAX on the CD.

Looping Animations

Perhaps the simplest motion-flow animation consists of one clip looped over and over again. This type of animation is useful for walk cycles and other repeating motion. The key to creating looping animation is to make sure that the pose adopted by the biped at the start of the loop cycle exactly matches the biped's pose at the end of the loop cycle. When hand-animating, you can best accomplish this match-up by using Copy and Paste Posture in the Copy/Paste rollout. When you already have a BIP file to work with, you can use the Motion Flow tools (or Motion Mixer) to loop your animation.

EXERCISE 10.7

Looping with Motion Flow

In this exercise, you'll create a walk cycle using the Motion Flow tools.

1. Load the file HAPPYDOGWALKLOOP.MAX from the CD.

   This file contains a 60-frame animation of three steps of a dog's walk, similar to the one created in the Chapter 7 exercise "Walking the Dog." In this walk sequence, the dog starts out from a walking pose. The dog's pose on frame 40 is the same as it is on frame 0. On frame 60, it matches frame 20. This gives us 20 frames of leeway between frames 40 and 60 for making a good transition.

2. Select any part of the biped and go to the Motion panel.

3. Click ▣ Save File, and save the file as HAPPYDOGWALK.BIP.

We'll use this BIP file to create a Motion Flow script. The original animation will be replaced by the motion in the script.

4. Click ▣ Motion Flow Mode.

5. Click ▣ Show Graph.

6. Click ▣ Create Multiple Clips, and choose DOGWALK.BIP.

7. Click ▣ Define Script.

8. Click twice on the DOGWALK clip in the Motion Flow Graph.

A transition is created on the graph from the DOGWALK clip to itself.

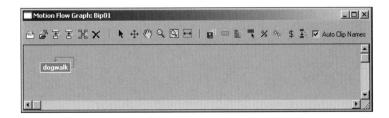

9. Click ⊞ Define Script again to turn it off.

10. Highlight the first DOGWALK clip listed on the Motion Flow Script rollout.

11. Click ⊞ Edit Transition on the Motion Flow Script rollout.

12. In the transition editor, change Length to 20.

13. For the Source Clip, change the Start frame to 40.

   Since we know that the current poses for the transition are at frame 40, there is no need to use any of the automatic tools. We can just set these numbers manually.

14. Click OK to close the transition editor.

   Play the animation to see the dog's walk looping.

Continue the Loop

You can now append as many DOGWALK clips to the script as you like in order to make the motion last longer.

1. Click ⊞ Define Script.

2. Choose "Append to end of script" and click OK.

3. Click twice again on the HAPPYDOGWALK clip.

   You'll see the length of the animation increase as you add the clip to the script.

4. Click ⊞ Define Script again to turn it off.

5. Close the Motion Flow Graph.

6. Play the animation.

   The dog now walks continuously throughout 180 frames. If you like, hide the biped and unhide the dog parts to see the dog mesh in action.

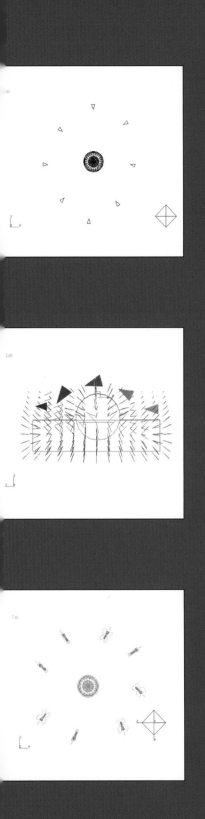

CHAPTER 11

Basic Crowds

A series of objects or bipeds can be made to move as a crowd does. Members of a crowd generally do the same actions, but not at the same time, in the same order, or at the same speed.

For example, consider a crowd of people walking around at an indoor shopping mall. Most people are moving in one of two directions. Most are walking at a slow or moderate pace, while a few move quickly. For the most part, people behave politely if someone's in the way, by either moving around them or stopping to let them pass.

You can animate any group of objects with Character Studio's Crowd tools. Whether they walk, fly, or swim, the same principle applies—the objects move similarly but not identically.

Crowds Overview

A scene animated with Crowd tools is called a *crowd simulation*. It's created with two types of helper objects: a Crowd helper and Delegate helpers. There is always just one Crowd helper in a simulation, and it controls the entire simulation. There can be one or more Delegate helpers, and usually there are several.

Delegates are made to follow *behaviors*, which are rules that govern the delegates' movement. For example, one type of behavior makes delegates move toward (or *seek*) a particular object, and another behavior prevents delegates from bumping into one another. It's common to combine behaviors so that, for example, delegates don't collide while seeking an object.

It's also possible to establish several sets of behaviors and cause delegates to change behavior according to conditions you specify. This is accomplished with simple MAXScripts called *cognitive controllers,* which you'll learn more about in Chapter 12.

After behaviors are assigned, the scene is *solved.* Solving the simulation means Character Studio goes through the animation frame by frame and determines what each delegate should be doing at each frame. Keys are assigned to delegates during this process.

An object or biped is then linked to each delegate, and the final scene can be rendered.

Often, objects linked to delegates are already animated; for example, a bird object might have flapping wings. If you simply made copies of the bird and linked them to delegates, all the birds would flap their wings at the same time. Instead, you can set up the bird animation so that in a certain number of frames, say 0–30, the wings are flapping, and in the rest, say 31–60, they aren't. Then you can use *animation states* (more about this in

Chapter 12) to tell the bird to use one part of the animation or another depending on certain parameters of the delegate.

Moths are a good example of crowd behavior. They seek a light source and fly around it, but when they get too close to it, they back off a bit, then come at it again. The moth can fly fast or slowly, sometimes coming nearly to a stop. It also tends to change direction quickly and frequently, and it has enough sense to avoid flying into other moths.

For most of the exercises in this chapter, we'll use our understanding of moths' behavior to choose the right behaviors for the crowd simulation.

Crowd Setup

To begin creating a crowd simulation, first you'll set up Crowd and Delegate helper objects. These helpers are available from the Helpers category of the Create panel.

To create a Crowd helper, simply click Crowd and then click and drag in the viewport. The Crowd helper is a green diamond-shaped object; its size doesn't affect the crowd simulation, but a large Crowd helper can be easier to see and select in the scene. Like other helper objects, Crowd helpers do not render.

To create a delegate, click Delegate and then click and drag. A delegate is a pyramid-shaped object. You will most likely want to have more than one delegate in a crowd simulation. Delegates can be cloned like any other object to make more copies.

Once the Delegates are created, you assign behaviors to them, via the Crowd helper.

> ►QUICKLIST◄
>
> **CROWD SIMULATIONS**
>
> 1. Create a Crowd helper.
> 2. Create delegates.
> 3. Select and assign behaviors.
> 4. Link bipeds or objects to delegates.
> 5. Solve the simulation.

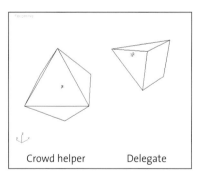

Crowd helper   Delegate

Behaviors

A *behavior* is a set of instructions that tell a delegate how to move. Typically, two or more behaviors are used together in the same simulation.

To set up a behavior, select the Crowd helper and go to the Setup rollout on the Modify panel. Click New in the Behaviors section, and choose a behavior from the list that appears.

After a behavior is selected, a rollout for it appears on the command panel. Use the options on this rollout to further set up the behavior. For example, the Seek Behavior rollout has buttons for choosing the object or objects to seek.

COMMON BEHAVIORS

Behavior	Result
Seek	The delegate approaches a specific object or objects.
Avoid	The delegate turns away or stops when it gets close to a particular object, or to another delegate.
Wander	The delegate moves aimlessly for a specific time period.
Surface Follow	The delegate moves along the surface of an object, such as terrain.
Space Warp	The delegate flows around a specified object (used with the Vector Field Space Warp; see Exercise 11.3).
Wall Repel	The delegate turns away when within a specified distance from a grid object.

After behaviors have been set up, they must be assigned to delegates in order for you to see any action. Behaviors are assigned to delegates via the Crowd helper. Select the Crowd helper, and click ⬜ Behavior Assignments on the Setup rollout of the Modify panel. The Behavior Assignments and Teams dialog opens, where you can assign behaviors.

Although behaviors can be assigned to individual delegates, using *teams* (a designated collection of delegates) can make the crowd simulation easier to control. Instead of having to assign a behavior to each delegate individually, you can assign it to the entire team at once. Delegates can be added or removed from teams at any time.

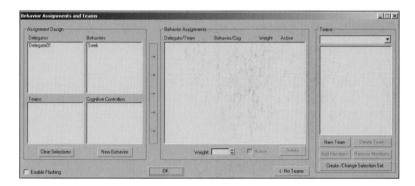

If the Teams section of the Behavior Assignments and Teams dialog is not visible, display it by clicking the Teams button under the Behavior Assignments section of the dialog. When the Teams section is visible, the Teams button becomes a No Teams button.

To set up a team, click New Team, and choose the desired delegates from the list. Then assign a behavior by selecting the team name and the behavior, and clicking the vertical bar of arrows between the Assignment Design and Behavior Assignments sections. (This bar only becomes available when both a behavior and a delegate or team are selected.)

After you have set up behaviors and assigned them to delegates, you must instruct Character Studio to solve the simulation. Solving the animation is very easy to do—just select the Crowd helper and then click Solve in the Solve rollout of the Modify panel. After a few moments, the simulation is calculated and you can play it. Usually, a simulation must be solved more than once to get it right. You can change behavior parameters or other settings and solve again as many times as you like.

EXERCISE 11.1

Creating a Simple Crowd Scene

In this exercise, you'll create a simple crowd scene simulating moths flying around a light source. Delegates will fly around a lamp object, and you'll become familiar with the Crowd tools. In later exercises, we'll show you how to use several behaviors and other tools together to make a complete simulation.

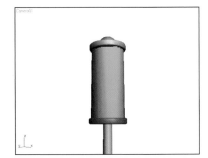

1. Load the file Moths.max from the CD. This scene contains a simple outdoor lamp, like one that might be found in a back-yard garden.

2. Zoom out of the Top viewport until the lamp is about 1/8 the size of the viewport.

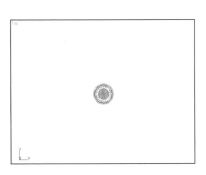

3. Go to the Create panel and click [icon] Helpers.

4. Click Crowd in the Helpers category of the Create panel. If you don't see the Crowd helper, make sure you are looking at the Standard Helpers, rather than any of the other seven categories of helper objects.

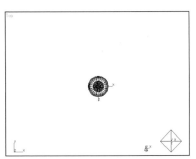

5. In the lower-right corner of the Top viewport, click and drag to create a Crowd helper about the same size as the lamp.

Create Delegates

1. Click Delegate in the Helpers category of the Create panel.

2. In the Top viewport, next to the Crowd helper, click and drag to create a delegate with a Width and Height of about 20 units, and a Depth of 30.

3. With the delegate selected, go to the Modify panel's Motion Parameters rollout.

   There are several settings for the delegate helper on the Motion Parameters rollout. Notice the series of checkboxes near the top of the rollout.

4. Uncheck the Constrain to XY Plane checkbox.

   By default, Constrain to XY Plane is checked, which will force the delegate to stay on the XY construction plane throughout the simulation. Since the moths are flying, we don't want this constraint, so we uncheck this setting before making copies of the delegate.

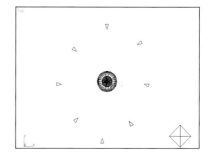

5. In the Top viewport, create seven copies of the delegate anywhere in the viewport.

6. Arrange the delegates in the Top viewport in a rough circle around the lamp. Point each delegate toward the lamp (the long point of the triangle should be turned in the direction of the lamp).

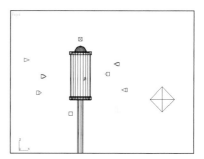

7. In the Front and Left viewports, move some of the delegates upward to randomize their positions.

Set Up Behaviors

Now that you have the helpers set up, you're ready to set up some behaviors. We'll start by setting up a behavior to make the delegates seek the lamp.

1. Select the Crowd helper.

2. On the Modify panel's Setup rollout, in the Behaviors section, click the New button.

3. Choose Seek Behavior from the list.

   A new rollout called Seek Behavior appears on the Modify panel.

4. Near the top of the Seek Behavior rollout, click the button labeled None, and then click on the center portion of the light (the part from which light will emit) in the Perspective viewport.

   The object name Light should appear on the button that you just clicked, indicating that this Seek behavior will target the Light object. Now you'll add these delegates to a team, and assign the Seek Behavior to the team.

5. On the Setup rollout, click [icon] Behavior Assignments.

   The Behavior Assignments and Teams dialog appears.

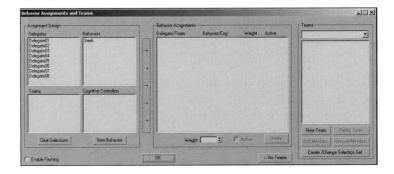

6. If the Teams area of the dialog is not displayed, click the Teams button at the bottom of the dialog under the Behavior Assignments section.

7. In the Teams area, click New Team. Select all eight delegates from the list that appears, and click OK.

   You have just created a team named Team0. Now you will use the left and middle parts of the Behavior Assignments and Teams dialog to assign a behavior to the team.

8. In the Teams list at the lower-left of the Assignment Design section, highlight the team name Team0.

9. In the Behaviors list at the upper-right of the Assignment Design section, highlight the Seek behavior.

   The vertical bar of arrows becomes available.

10. Click the vertical bar of arrows.

   The Seek behavior has been assigned to Teamo, as shown in the Behavior Assignments section.

11. Click OK on the dialog to close it.

Solve the Simulation

Now that one behavior has been assigned to the Teamo, you can solve the animation to see how the behavior works.

1. With the Crowd helper still selected, on the Modify panel, scroll down to the Solve rollout.

2. Click the Solve button.

   Wait a few moments while the simulation is solved. You can see the animation being generated frame by frame.

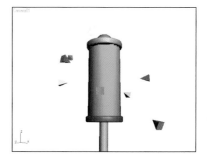

3. Play the animation.

   The delegates cluster around the light, crashing into one another and even passing through the light itself. To keep this from happening, we'll use an Avoid behavior.

Add Another Behavior

Even though the animation has been solved, you can add more behaviors to make the simulation more realistic. Next, you'll add an Avoid behavior to keep the moths from colliding, and then re-solve the animation.

1. Go to frame zero, then scroll up to the Setup rollout and click the New button. Choose Avoid Behavior.

   An Avoid Behavior rollout appears on the Modify panel.

2. Click the ![icon] Multiple Selection button on the Avoid Behavior rollout.

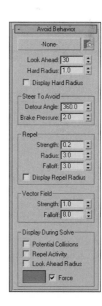

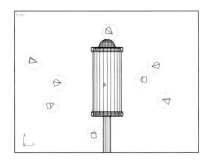

3. In the Select dialog, choose all the delegates and click Select.

4. On the Avoid Behavior rollout, check the Display Hard Radius checkbox. You'll see a Hard Radius gizmo appear around each delegate.

5. Change the Hard Radius amount by clicking and dragging on the spinner arrows. Set Hard Radius to 0.5. (In the figure the hard radius is set larger so you can see it clearly.)

   The Hard Radius is the "personal space" of the delegate. Each delegate will look ahead by a certain number of frames to see if it's going to crash into other delegates anytime in the near future. If so, it will turn to avoid the other delegates.

6. Click Behavior Assignments on the Setup rollout to open the Behavior Assignments and Teams dialog, and assign the Avoid behavior to the team.

7. On the Solve rollout, click Solve and wait for the simulation to be solved.

8. Play the animation.

   The delegates avoid one another while flying around the lamp. However, they still cluster around the center and sometimes fly through the lamp, all the while flying slowly and regularly. We will remedy these problems in the exercises that follow.

9. Save the scene in your folder as MyMoths01.max.

Changing Multiple Delegates

At this point, the delegates move more slowly than real moths would. If you only wanted to change this situation for one delegate, you could select the delegate and go to the Modify panel. Under the Speed section of the Motion Parameters rollout, the

Average Speed parameter sets the delegate's velocity throughout the simulation.

For our purposes, however, we want to change the Average Speed parameters for a team of cloned delegates. Using the Modify panel to change parameters for each individual delegate could become very time consuming and tedious. Instead, you can select the Crowd helper, and on the Modify panel's Setup rollout, click the ⊞ Multiple Delegate Editing button. The Edit Multiple Delegates dialog appears.

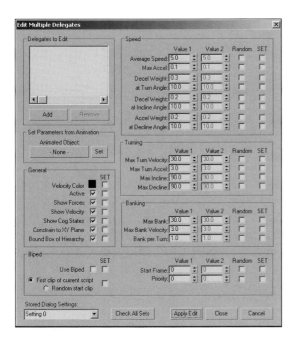

To choose the delegates for editing, click the Add button at the upper-left of the dialog and select them from the dialog that appears. Then make your changes, using the many entry fields and checkboxes available in the dialog. Notice that each parameter has a SET checkbox; check this to indicate that the parameter should be set to the new value when you click the Apply Edit button at the bottom of the dialog.

The Edit Multiple Delegates dialog contains some options that the Modify panel does not have. For example, you can check the Random checkbox for any of the speed, banking, and turning values and enter a range for the value. Each delegate will then have a different value within the range. This feature is very useful for making a simulation look more natural.

EXERCISE 11.2

Speeding Up the Delegates

In this exercise, you'll improve on the last scene you made by first extending the animation, and then making the delegates fly faster.

1. Continue using your work from the preceding exercise, or load the file MyMoths01.max from your folder or Moths01.max from the CD.

2. In the Animation playback controls, click ⬚ Time Configuration, and set the Length to 200. Click OK to close the dialog.

   In order for the simulation to be solved for the entire animation, you must add the new frames to the End Solve parameter.

3. Select the Crowd helper and go to the Modify panel.

4. On the Solve rollout, change End Solve to 200.

   Now the simulation will be solved for all frames, both the original and the newly added.

Edit Delegates

1. With the Crowd helper still selected, go to the Modify panel. In the Setup rollout, click ⬚ Multiple Delegate Editing.

▶TIP◀

If you have already solved a simulation for a number of frames and don't need it to be solved again for those frames, you can change the Start Solve parameter to a later frame number. The Simulation Start value tells Character Studio when to start moving the delegates around. If you want the simulation to start at frame 30, for example, set both Start Solve and Simulation Start to 30.

The Edit Multiple Delegates dialog appears.

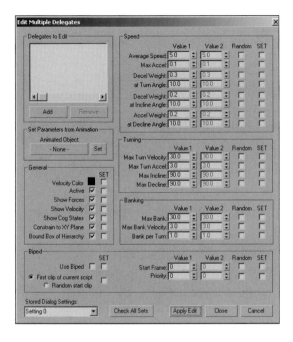

2. If the Delegates to Edit list is empty, do the following; otherwise, continue with step 3:

   At the upper-left of the dialog, click Add, and select all the delegates from the dialog that appears.

3. In the Speed section, next to Average Speed, check the Random checkbox.

   Note that Value 2 is now available.

4. Change Value 1 to 10.

5. Change Value 2 to 50.

6. Check the SET checkbox for Average Speed, to ensure that the values will actually be set.

7. Click Apply Edit at the bottom of the dialog to apply the edits and close the dialog.

8. On the Solve rollout, click Solve.

   The simulation is re-solved from the beginning and includes the frames you added. The delegates now move more erratically, as real moths do. However, they still pass through the object. This problem will be fixed in later exercises.

9. Save the scene in your folder as `MyMoths02.max`.

Making a Vector Field Space Warp

To make delegates fly around an object without passing through it, you combine the Space Warp Behavior with the *Vector Field Space Warp*. The Vector Field Space Warp sets up a field of *vectors* (lines or arrows) in the directions of a selected object's face normals. When the Vector Field Space Warp is used to define a Space Warp behavior, the delegates will tend to move in a direction perpendicular to the nearest flow line.

When this behavior is used in conjunction with a Seek and an Avoid Behavior, delegates will continually fly around an object without penetrating it.

A Vector Field Space Warp is actually box-shaped. This box is called a *lattice*. The flow lines are created by picking an object that sits within the space warp. Vectors are then created in the directions of the chosen object's face normals.

The frequency of vectors determines how often delegates will be affected. This frequency is set by the density of segments in the Vector Field Space Warp, not by the amount of detail on the chosen object.

Change Length Segs, Width Segs, and Height Segs to change the segments on the lattice. The number of segments determines the frequency of the vectors. Higher values will give you a denser Vector Field that will in turn affect the delegates more frequently—but it will also add time to solving the simulation. Generally, values between 10 and 20 give excellent results without yielding a long solution time.

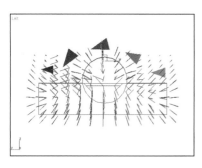

Before you designate the object to define the space warp, it's usually a good idea to use Align to align the lattice with the object. Then pick the object by going to the Compute Vectors section of the Obstacle Parameters rollout. Click the button under Vector Field Object, and choose the object that will be used to generate the vectors. The object name then appears on the button.

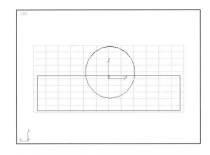

The Range parameter in Compute Vectors sets the area in which the Vector Field will be generated. If the chosen object is smaller than the Vector Field area, you'll want to increase this value to encompass the entire area that you want affected. Vectors will be generated only in areas of the range that are encompassed by the lattice.

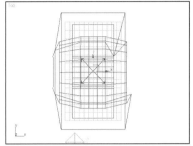

The vector field is now completely set up. Click the Compute button to create the vectors, and wait a few moments for the computation to complete. To see the vectors, check the Show Vector Field checkbox on the Obstacle Parameters rollout to see the vectors.

Vectors appear as small blue lines. If they aren't visible, try increasing the Vector Scale parameter in the Display section near the top of the Obstacle Parameters rollout (to 25, 50, or 100). This value does not change the effect of the vectors, but simply makes them easier to see in viewports.

> **►NOTE◄**
>
> Only objects with no modifiers applied to them will be available for designation as a Vector Field Space Warp object. If the desired object has modifiers applied to it, collapse the object's modifier stack before attempting to designate the object.

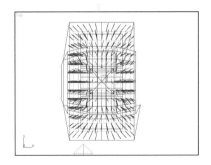

Once you've successfully made the Vector Field, you can check or uncheck the Display section's Show Lattice and Show Range checkboxes to unclutter your screen. You might want to leave Show Vector Field checked so that you can watch the delegates react to the vectors during the simulation solution.

If you like, you can hide the chosen Vector Field object without affecting the crowd simulation.

Defining the Space Warp Behavior

Once the Vector Field Space Warp has been set up, it's a simple matter to use it to define a Space Warp behavior.

Select the Crowd helper and go to the Modify panel. Click the New button on the Setup rollout, and choose Space Warp Behavior.

On the Space Warp Behavior rollout, click the button labeled None, and pick the Vector Field Space Warp. If it's difficult to pick the Space Warp directly from the screen, you can select it from a list by pressing the H key on the keyboard.

Notice that the Space Warp Behavior has only one parameter, Display Force, which is used for display only. Settings that affect the strength, direction, and other aspects of the Vector Field are all set on the Vector Field itself, not on the Space Warp Behavior.

As with all behaviors, the Space Warp behavior must be assigned to a team by clicking ⬚ Behavior Assignments on the Setup rollout. After that, you can click Solve to see how well the Space Warp behavior works with other behaviors assigned to delegates.

EXERCISE 11.3

Setting Up a Vector Field for Moths

In this exercise, you'll set up a Vector Field Space Warp and use it with the Space Warp behavior, to push delegates around the object. Since the delegates already have a Seek behavior telling them to seek the object, and an Avoid behavior telling them to avoid one another, the result should be that they fly around and around the object without penetrating it.

This setup causes delegates to alternately approach the object and back off from it. Sounds like the way moths behave, doesn't it? This trio of behaviors—Seek, Avoid, and Space Warp—is very handy for simulations of insects, birds, airplanes, spaceships, and other flying objects. Refinements for the delegates, such as speed, whether they fly erratically or smoothly, the strength of their approach and retreat, and how much space is kept between them can all be adjusted with various behavior and delegate parameters.

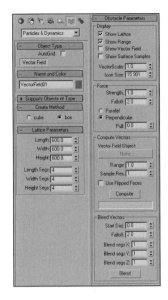

1. Load the file MyMoths02.max from your folder, or load the file Moths02.max from CD.

2. Go to the Create panel and click ▓ Space Warps. Choose Particles & Dynamics from the drop-down list.

3. Click Vector Field.

4. In the Top viewport, create a Vector Field of any size. Click and drag to define the Length and Width, and then drag upward and click to set the Height of the lattice.

5. On the Create panel, change the lattice's Length, Width, and Height parameters to 600.

6. In the Lattice Parameters rollout, change Length Segs, Width Segs, and Height Segs to 10.

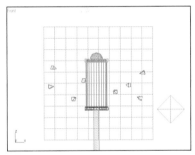

7. Use Align to align the center of the Vector Field Space Warp with the center of the Light object.

8. Select the Vector Field and go to the Modify panel.

9. In the Compute Vectors section, click the button under Vector Field Object and pick the object Light.

   The object name Light should now appear on the button.

10. Increase the Range parameter to 200.

    The range appears as an olive-green wireframe extending out from the Light object. Notice that nearly the entire range is encompassed by the lattice.

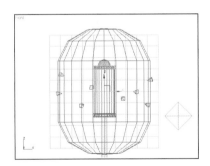

11. In the Display section, uncheck the Show Lattice checkbox so that you can more easily see the Vector Field.

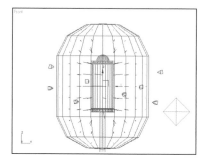

12. In the Compute Vectors section, increase the Range to 240. Then click Compute to create the Vector Field.

13. In the Display section, check the Show Vector Field checkbox.

14. Increase VectorScale to 50 in order to better see the vectors.

Set the Space Warp Behavior

Now that the Vector Field is set up, you can create and assign the Space Warp behavior that will make the moths follow the warp.

1. Select the Crowd helper, go to the Modify panel's Setup rollout, and click New.

2. Choose the Space Warp Behavior.

3. On the Space Warp Behavior rollout, click the button labeled None.

4. Press the H key and choose VectorField01 from the dialog that appears.

5. On the Setup rollout, click ⬀ Behavior Assignments.

6. Assign the Space Warp behavior to Team0, and click OK to close the dialog.

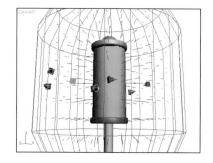

7. On the Solve rollout, click Solve.

   When the simulation has been solved, you will see the delegates fly around and around the lamp without flying through it. One or two delegates might still fly through, but most of them will avoid crashing into the light. In later exercises, you'll learn how to adjust parameters for the Space Warp and Avoid behaviors to get the best results with this particular simulation.

8. Press the H key to select the Vector field, then hide the Vector Field object.

9. Save the scene as MyMoths03.max in your folder.

One problem with the simulation at this point is that the delegates end up flying around the same area, practically in single file. This is largely due to the regularity of the Vector Field. The Light object is a nice, clean, straight cylinder, which looks great as a light but doesn't make the best Vector Field for a bunch of moths. The vectors are too regular and even, making the moths fly regularly and evenly. But real moths fly erratically, changing direction frequently. So our moths will do better with vectors that go in all directions. To achieve this, we need to use an object with irregular faces, something about the same size and shape as the Light but with faces angled in all directions.

EXERCISE 11.4

Varying Vector Direction for the Moths

In this exercise, you'll change the object of the Vector Field Space Warp from the nice, regular Light to an irregular object. This will generate irregular vectors, causing the moths to move more erratically.

1. Load the file MyMoths03.max from your folder, or load the file Moths03.max from the CD.

2. Unhide the object Mangled Light.

   This is a ChamferCyl object to which the Noise modifier has been applied. Quite a different Vector Field will result from designated this object for vectors. Before we can use it, however, we must collapse the object's modifier stack so that it can be picked for the Vector Field Space Warp. Before collapsing the object, let's make a copy in case we need to make changes to it later.

3. Create a copy of the object Mangled Light, and call it Mangled Light Copy.

4. Hide the object Mangled Light.

5. Select the object Mangled Light Copy.

6. On the Modify panel, in the Modifier Stack rollout, click Noise so that you're at the top of the stack.

7. Right-click and select Collapse All. If a warning message appears, click Yes to go ahead with the collapse operation.

Change the Vector Object

1. Unhide and select VectorField01, the Vector Field Space Warp.

2. Click the button under Vector Field Object that is currently labeled Light, press the H key, and pick the object Mangled Light.

   The object name Mangled Light should now appear on the button.

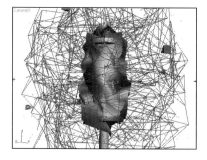

3. Click Compute to recompute the Vector Field.

   The vectors now go every which way, and so will the delegates.

4. Hide the Vector Field and the object Mangled Light.

5. Select the Crowd helper; then on the Solve rollout, click Solve.

   The delegates now fly around much more erratically.

6. Save the scene as `MyMoths04.max` in your folder.

Once you've solved a simulation that utilizes a Space Warp behavior and a Vector Field Space Warp, you'll usually need to make a few adjustments. All changes to this behavior must be made by selecting the Vector Field Space Warp and going to the Modify panel.

USEFUL VECTOR FIELD SETTINGS

Parameter	Result
Strength	Higher values cause vectors to affect delegates more, which can cause the Space Warp behavior to have more of an effect than other behaviors. Changing the Strength parameter changes the lengths of vectors onscreen.
Pull	Higher values pull the delegates in toward the space warp, while negative values push delegates away. Increase the Pull value when delegates have a tendency to drift away from the space warp, or change it to a negative number when they seem to drift toward the space warp.
Falloff	Higher values cause vectors at the outer edge of the range to have less effect than those near the center. Sometimes, higher values such as 8 or 15 will give a simulation a more realistic look.
Avoid Behavior	Used with a Vector Field Space Warp, the Avoid behavior can make use of the Vector Field to force objects away from the space warp itself. On the Avoid Behavior rollout, the settings in the Vector Field section control this type of avoidance. The Vector Field Strength and Falloff help control the degree of avoidance.

Behavior Weights

Another tool you have for controlling delegate actions is the Weight value assigned to each behavior. When behaviors are assigned to delegates or teams on the Behavior Assignments and Teams dialog, each behavior/team pair is assigned a Weight of 1.0 by default. This means that all behaviors initially have the same weight (influence) on the simulation. If you lower a behavior's Weight, it will have less influence on delegates.

Weight values can range from 0.0 (no effect) to 1.0 (highest precedence). Setting the Weight to 0.0 is the same as removing the behavior from the team assignment.

For example, if delegates are getting too close to the Seek object, you can reduce the Weight setting of the Seek behavior. In this way, other behaviors with higher Weight values will take precedence, and delegates may be less likely to get close to or crash through the Seek object.

To change a behavior's Weight value, select the Crowd helper and go to the Modify panel. Click [icon] Behavior Assignments. In the Behavior Assignments and Teams dialog, select the team/behavior pair in the Behavior Assignments section. The Weight parameter will become available at the bottom of the dialog. Type in a new Weight value and press Enter. Click OK to exit the dialog. The new Weight value will be used the next time you solve the simulation.

EXERCISE 11.5

Refining the Moth Vector Field

Now that you've seen the basics of the behaviors, you can refine their parameters and change their weighting to make the moth simulation more realistic.

1. Load the file MyMoths04.max from your folder, or load the file Moths04.max from the CD.

2. Right-click in the viewport, choose Unhide by Name, and unhide the Vector Field.

3. Select the Vector Field and go to the Modify panel. In the Obstacle Parameters rollout, in the Force section, set the Strength parameter to 10. You'll see the vectors elongate in the viewport.

4. Hide the Vector Field.

5. Select the Crowd helper.

6. On the Setup rollout, choose the Avoid Behavior from the pulldown list.

7. On the Avoid Behavior rollout, in the Vector Field section, change Falloff to 22.

8. On the Setup rollout, click [icon] Behavior Assignments.

9. Select the Teamo/Seek Behavior assignment from the Behavior Assignments section of the dialog.

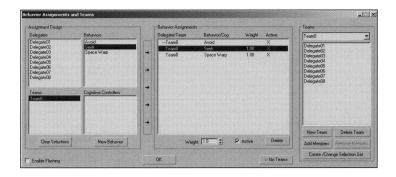

10. Change the Weight parameter to 0.5.

    How did I arrive at these numbers? The big secret is... trial and error. It's not unusual to solve a simulation 10, 20, or 50 times before it's exactly right. That's what I did, trying various parameter settings until the simulation shaped up.

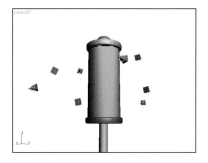

11. Click OK to close the Behavior Assignments and Teams dialog, and click Solve to solve the simulation.

    The delegates now keep their distance from the light.

12. Save the scene as MyMoths05.max in your folder.

Simulation Troubleshooting Tips

When you're doing simulations, what you're looking for is the simplest setup. Simple means fewer behaviors, and thus fewer parameters to worry about. The trick is not to waste time trying combinations that won't ever work. This is a sure time-waster!

It's easy to get caught up in setting various parameters all over the place to get the simulation to look right, especially when you consider that similar animation can be created with completely different behaviors. When creating this series of exercises, I went through a number of permutations before striking on the simplest one that would work.

At one point, I had a Repel behavior on the Light object to keep the delegates away. This worked well, but the animation without it looked better to me. To prevent the delegates from congregating around the middle of the light, I tried placing three small boxes inside the Light object and using them as multiple Seek objects. The simulation looks fine with this setup—different, but just as good. After I placed the radical, mangled Vector Field object, I changed the Seek object back to the Light object, and it all looked fine that way, too. The point is that a different yet just-as-good simulation can be achieved in a number of ways.

To save time, use these guidelines when setting up simulations:

- *Assign behaviors.* Make sure you assign each behavior to delegates before solving! This is an obvious necessity, but it's worth mentioning again. A missing assignment is the first thing to look for when the behavior isn't having an effect on your simulation.

- *Less is more.* Avoid adding more and more behaviors to get one team to behave. I have never needed more than six behaviors for one team, and three to five is the norm. If you need more than six behaviors, it's likely that some of them aren't helping out at all and could even be interfering with the result. It's easy to unassign and reassign behaviors in the Behavior Assignments and Teams dialog, so simply unassign unwanted behaviors rather than delete them.

- *Make big changes.* If you keep making changes and don't see any effect, don't be afraid to crank any of the Strength parameters up high, or reduce Brake Pressure in the Avoid behavior to near zero. If doing this has no effect on the simulation, then the behavior either hasn't been assigned or just isn't having an effect, in which case it should be unassigned. If extreme settings do have a radical effect, you can always set the parameters back closer to their original values and solve again. Just be sure to note the original values before making a big change!

- *Start over.* Sometimes you'll want to get rid of all the delegate animation and solve from scratch. Choose File > New from the menu, and in the New Scene dialog select Keep Objects and Hierarchy. This removes all animation keys while keeping all your objects and behavior assignments intact.

When Good Delegates Go Bad

At times, a simulation will work perfectly except for one or two delegates that insist on flying right through the Vector Field object or flinging themselves out into space, never to be seen again. No matter which parameters you change or behaviors you add, these "bad" delegates refuse to stick with the program.

When this happens, you can drive yourself crazy trying to get the simulation to work for every single delegate, or you can be sensible and use this easy solution.

1. Create a few extra delegates when setting up a simulation. A good rule of thumb is to create 10–20 percent more delegates than you actually need. If you need 10, make 11 or 12; if you need 100, make 110–120.

2. Work on the simulation until *most* of the delegates are performing perfectly.

3. When you're sure the simulation has been solved for the last time, delete the delegates that aren't behaving correctly.

That's it, problem solved!

One word of caution: If you delete a few delegates and then later decide to re-solve, the simulation will change to some degree. Delegates that moved in a certain way in order to avoid deleted delegates will now move differently. This may or may not be a problem, depending on your simulation, so just keep an eye out.

Any one delegate is not bad by nature, so deleting it while you're still doing solve operations won't get rid of the problem. It's very likely that another delegate will simply take the bad one's place and be bad, as well.

Linking Objects to Delegates

Once the delegates are moving as planned, you can link objects to delegates to make them move as the delegates move. Ordinary linking is used, but Character Studio has tools to make it easy to align objects with delegates and link them together.

Before linking objects to delegates, make sure the objects' local Y axes are pointing in the direction that you consider "forward" for the object. Character Studio's automatic alignment tools always align objects' local Y axes with the direction in which the delegates point.

> **►TIP◄**
>
> After you align and link objects to delegates, you can still make changes to the simulation and solve it. This will work even if delegates are hidden. The linked objects will move with the delegates in the new animation.

Once the objects are linked to the delegates, the objects will move along with the delegates when you play the animation. Hide the delegates, and the linked objects will continue to move as the delegates do. You're now ready to render the scene.

Aligning and Linking Moths

Now that our simulation is refined, we can add the moths and see the result. First we'll align the moths to the delegates, so they'll fly in the proper direction.

1. Load the file MyMoths05.max from your folder, or load the file Moths05.max from the CD.

2. Unhide the grouped objects.

   Eight moths appear in the scene. Play the animation and you'll see them beat their wings. Their flapping does no good, however; they remain stationary.

3. Select the Crowd helper and go to the Modify panel.

4. On the Setup rollout, click 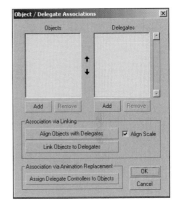 Object/Delegate Associations.

   The Object/Delegate Associations dialog appears.

5. Click the Add button under the Objects list. Choose the objects.

6. Click the Add button under the Delegates list, and select all the delegates.

7. Click Align Objects with Delegates.

   The moths are now aligned with the delegates, in the same order in which they're listed in the dialog.

8. Click Link Objects to Delegates.

   The objects are now linked to the delegates.

9. Click OK to close the dialog.

10. Hide all the delegates.

11. Play the animation. The moths beat their wings as they fly around the lamp.

12. Save your work as MyMoths6.max.

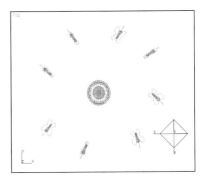

Scatter Tool

When placing delegates, you have the option of cloning them individually, or scattering them across a surface. The Scatter feature is useful for placing delegates on an irregular surface.

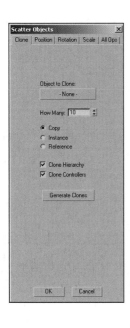

To scatter delegates, select the Crowd helper and click  Scatter in the Setup rollout of the Modify panel. The Scatter Objects dialog appears.

On the Clone tab, you can specify the number and type of clones. On the Position tab, you can choose the object over which to scatter the delegates. The Rotation tab specifies the facing directions of delegates, and the Scale tab sets the scale.

The All Ops tab is where you make the scattering happen. When Clones is checked in this tab, the clones are generated. If you don't like the way the clones are placed, you can return to the All Ops tab to try different configurations. When the Inc Seed checkbox is checked for the Positions, Rotations, and/or Scales operations, you can click Scatter repeatedly to generate new arrangements of delegates. Once the initial clones are placed, it's best to uncheck Clones. Otherwise, more clones will be made.

EXERCISE 11.7

Scattering Delegates

In this exercise, you'll use the Scatter tool to place delegates on an irregular surface. In the next chapter, these delegates will become birds that peck at the ground for a while and then fly away.

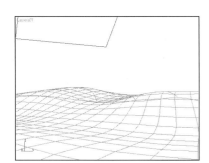

1. Load the file Hill.max from the CD.

   This file contains a scene with a small hill. A Crowd helper and one delegate have already been created. A grid has been placed in the sky to be used as a Seek object.

2. Select the Crowd helper and go to the Modify panel.

3. On the Setup rollout, click ⊞ Scatter to open the Scatter Objects dialog.

4. On the Clone tab, under Object to Clone, click the button and choose Delegate01.

5. For How Many, enter 14.

6. Click the Position tab.

7. For Placement relative to Object, change from On Grid to On Surface.

8. Under Grid/Box/Sphere/Surface/Shape, click the button and choose the object Patch for Delegates.

   This patch is a small area that shows in the left side of the camera view. We'll use this patch as a basis for scattering the delegates.

9. Set Offset to 10. This will scatter the delegates 10 units offset from the patch.

10. Click the Rotation tab.

11. Under Look At Target, set Sideways Deviation to 60.

    This will turn the delegates by random angles, up to 60 degrees off the current delegate angle.

12. Click the All Ops tab.

13. Check the Compute checkboxes for Clones, Positions, and Rotations.

14. Click Scatter.

    In the camera view, you'll see delegates scattered over the hillside.

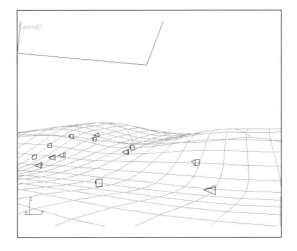

►TIP◄

After you click Scatter, if it looks like there are twice as many clones, you may be experiencing a redraw problem. Click OK to close the Scatter dialog, then maximize the viewport and then minimize it with Alt+W, and the old delegates should disappear.

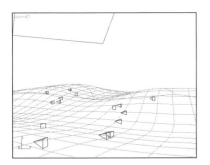

15. Check the Inc Seed checkboxes for Positions and Rotations.

16. Click Scatter again.

    The delegates are now arranged differently.

17. Click Scatter as many times as you like until you're satisfied with the distribution of delegates.

    For this exercise, simply choose an arrangement where they're all visible in the camera view, and spaced apart rather than on top of one another. Shown here is the arrangement we chose.

18. Click OK to close the Scatter Objects dialog.

19. Save the scene as Hill01.max in your folder.

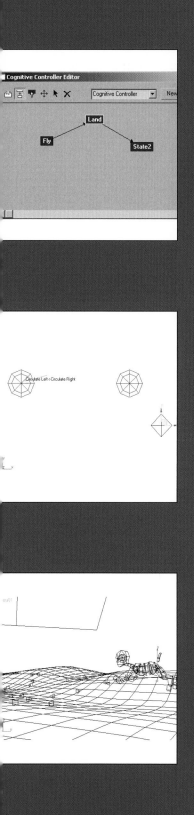

CHAPTER 12

Complex Crowds

With 3ds Max 8, it's possible to make delegates follow one set of behaviors and then switch to another set of behaviors based on certain conditions. The tool required to do this type of animation is called a cognitive controller.

In this chapter, you'll learn how to further refine your crowd simulations using simple MAXScripts. Finally, you'll use animation states to make the delegates use different animation for different motions.

Cognitive Controllers

A cognitive controller is represented as a graph with *states* and *transitions*. A *state* consists of a set of behaviors. Between states are *transitions* from one state to another. The transition goes in the direction of the transition arrow.

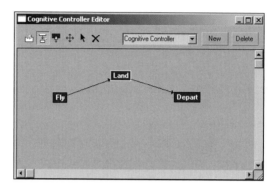

Each transition includes, as part of its definition, a test to determine whether a delegate should pass from one state to another. The test is enacted by a simple MAXScript. Even if you've never written a MAXScript before, you'll find that the short scripts required for cognitive controllers are quite easy to write and use.

Setting Up Cognitive Controllers

Before using cognitive controllers, you must first set up a Crowd helper, delegates, and two or more behaviors (as you did in Chapter 11, "Basic Crowds"). Although it's not strictly necessary to set up behaviors and solve the simulation before using cognitive controllers, doing some solving is helpful to ensure that the behaviors are working the way you want them to.

Let's get started working with the Cognitive Controller Editor. Select the Crowd helper and go to the Modify panel. On the Setup rollout, click Cognitive Controllers. This opens the Cognitive Controller Editor, which works something like the Motion Flow Graph. You set up states, and then establish transitions between them.

Click New, and then click in two or more areas of the graph to create *state holders*. These boxes represent animation behaviors, similar to the clips in the Motion Flow Graph.

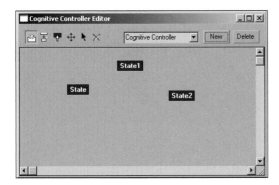

Click [icon] Select State/Transition and then right-click a state holder. This opens a dialog for setting up and editing the state.

In the top field of the State dialog, you can change the default State to a more meaningful name. Then click Add, and choose the behaviors that define the state. When you're finished, close the dialog by clicking the X at the upper-right of the dialog. The new state name appears on the state holder in the editor. You set up each of the other states in the same way.

Once the states are established, you can create transitions between them. To do so, click [icon] Create Transition and then click and drag from one state to another to create a transition in that direction.

►TIP◄

Take care to click *and* drag when creating a transition—if you simply click, you'll create a transition from the state to itself.

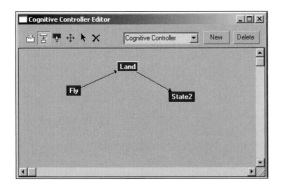

To begin setting up the transition, right-click on a transition line. This opens a dialog for setting up and editing the transition.

Here you can set various parameters that are by now familiar, such as the Duration of the transition. This transition editor is also where you specify the conditions under which the transition will occur. Under Transition Condition, enter the name of the MAXScript function you wish to use. This can be any function name without spaces. Each transition function must have a unique name. Then you click Edit MAXScript to open the MAXScript window, and type in the MAXScript.

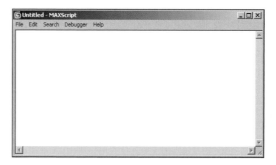

Creating the Transition Script

As mentioned earlier, each transition includes a test to see whether a delegate should use the transition or stay in its current state. Every delegate is tested at every frame.

Usually, the test checks whether a parameter is above or below a specific value. There are a number of parameters you can use for the test:

- *Proximity* of a delegate to other objects (in units)

- *Speed* of the delegate (in units per frame)

- *Condition* of another parameter in the scene (for example, the radius of an object)

- *Position* of the delegate (X, Y, or Z position in units)

- *Duration* of the current state (number of frames)

Let's examine a short example of a transition MAXScript in order to study its required contents. The following brief MAXScript tests how long a delegate has been in its current state, and performs the transition if the duration is longer than 50 frames.

```
fn Trans1 del t = (
  if del.duration > 50 then 1 else 0
)
```

The first line of a transition script

```
fn Trans1 del t = (
```

is always the same. It signals the beginning of a MAXScript function (fn), specifies the function name entered in the Transition Condition field of the transition editor (Trans1 in this example), and sets up the test. Here, del refers to the delegate, t is the current time in frame numbers in the simulation (used internally by cognitive controllers), and the characters = (denote the beginning of the test information.

The second line

```
if del.duration > 50 then 1 else 0
```

is the actual test. This test uses the variable del.duration to check the number of frames in which the delegate has been in its current state. If the delegate has been in the state more than 50 frames (> 50), the result is 1; otherwise, the result is 0. If the result is 1, the transition takes place. Otherwise, the delegate stays in the same state.

The final line contains just the parenthesis that closes the transition test and indicates that it's finished.

Once the script is written, you can close the MAXScript window by clicking the X in its upper-right corner. If you make an error in typing in the script, such as leaving out one of the parentheses, the window will not close. MAXScript will detect the error and highlight the line where it believes the error occurred.

When you've set up all the transitions you need, you can close the Cognitive Controller Editor and assign the cognitive controller to delegates. On the Setup rollout, click Behavior Assignments; then use the Behavior Assignments and Teams dialog to create a team of all delegates that will follow the cognitive controller.

In Behavior Assignments and Teams, the name you entered in the Cognitive Controller Editor will appear under Cognitive Controllers in the Assignment Design section. Select and assign the cognitive controller to teams the just same way you assigned behaviors. The assignment appears in the Behavior Assignments section of the dialog.

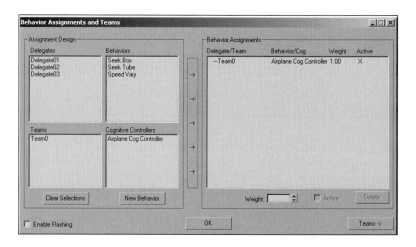

►NOTE◄

In order for the cognitive controller to work properly, you'll have to delete any behaviors previously assigned to the team. Simply highlight the behavior/team pair and click the Delete button at the bottom of the Behavior Assignments section.

Now you're ready to solve the animation. As the simulation is solving, text appears next to each delegate telling you which behavior the delegate is currently following. When the delegate is going through a transition, the transition information appears next to the delegate.

EXERCISE 12.1

Making a Simple Cognitive Controller

This exercise illustrates how to set up the simplest of cognitive controllers. The scene will contain one delegate that seeks one sphere first, then another. First you'll set up the behaviors; then you'll create the cognitive controller that determines when they are used. The purpose of this exercise is simply to familiarize you with the steps involved in setting up cognitive controllers. A later exercise will use a more complex setup.

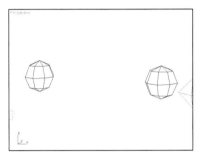

1. Load the file SimpleCog01.max from the CD.

   This scene contains two spheres, a delegate, and a Crowd helper.

2. Select the Crowd helper and go to the Modify panel.

   Just two behaviors are needed for this scene: one to seek the sphere on the left, and the other to seek the sphere on the right.

3. On the Setup rollout, click New. Choose Seek Behavior.

4. Change the name of the behavior from Seek to Seek Left Sphere.

5. On the Seek Behavior rollout, click the None button. In the Top viewport, click the sphere on the left to designate it as the sought object.

   The object name Sphere Left appears on the button.

6. On the Setup rollout, click New again, and choose Seek Behavior again.

7. Change the name of the behavior to Seek Right Sphere.

8. On the Seek Behavior rollout, click the None button, and click the sphere on the right.

Set Up the States

Now we're ready to set up the cognitive controllers, beginning with the states.

1. On the Setup rollout, click ⊞ Cognitive Controllers.

The Cognitive Controller Editor appears.

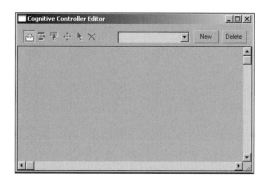

2. Click New, and the default name Cognitive Controller appears at the top of the editor. Replace it by entering the name Back and Forth.

3. Click twice in the editor to create two state holders.

   Notice that when you move the cursor over the graph, the cursor changes to an arrow with an asterisk at the end of it.

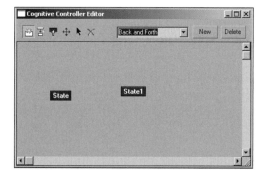

4. Click ![arrow] Select State/Transition.

5. Right-click the first state holder, and enter the name Circulate Left in the State dialog.

6. Click Add, and choose the Seek Left Sphere behavior.

   This state is now defined by the Seek Left Sphere behavior.

7. Click OK to close the Circulate Left dialog.

8. Right-click the second state holder, and enter the name Circulate Right in the State dialog.

9. Click Add, and choose the Seek Right Sphere behavior. Click OK to close the dialog.

Create the Transition

With the behavior states established, we can now create a transition between them.

1. In the Cognitive Controller Editor, click ▣ Create Transition.

2. Click and drag from the Circulate Left state to the Circulate Right state.

   The transition arrow appears on the editor between the two states.

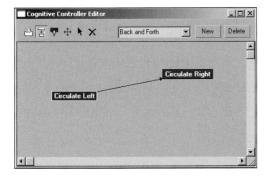

3. Click ▣ Select State/Transition.

4. Right-click on the transition line, and in the transition editor that appears, change Duration to 5.

5. Under Transition Condition, enter the name Trans1.

6. Click Edit MAXScript to open the MAXScript window.

7. Enter the following script in the window:

```
fn Trans1 del t = (
 if del.duration > 50 then 1 else 0
)
```

This tells the delegate to stay in its current state until it has been in that state for more than 50 frames, at which time it will switch to the other state.

8. Close the MAXScript window by clicking the X at the upper-right corner.

   If you made an error in typing in the script, such as leaving out one of the parentheses, the window will not close. MAXScript will detect the error and highlight the line where it believes the error occurred. If this happens, look carefully over your script and compare it with the script shown in step 7. When you've corrected the error, you can close the window.

9. Click OK to close the transition editor, and close the Cognitive Controller Editor by clicking the X at the upper-right corner.

10. On the Setup rollout, click ⬚ Behavior Assignments.

11. In the Behavior Assignments and Teams dialog, Assignment Design section, highlight Delegate01 in the Delegates list, and then Back and Forth in the Cognitive Controllers section. Click the vertical bar of arrows to assign the cognitive controller to the delegate.

12. Click OK to exit the dialog.

   The cognitive controller is all set up, and you can now solve the simulation.

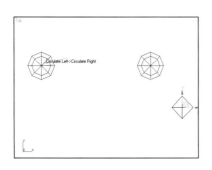

13. On the Solve rollout, click Solve.

   Wait a few moments while the simulation is solved. You'll see the delegate going from one state to the next, and the text describing its current state or transition.

14. Save the scene as `SimpleCog02.max` in your folder.

Circular Transitions

Sometimes you'll want to have transitions going both ways between two states, or to have transitions go in a circle between several states. The transitions are set up in the usual way, each with its own script to determine the conditions under which it will occur. The delegate will continue to cycle through the states according to the transition conditions until the final frame of the simulation is reached.

When you set up a circular transition, you must take care to set the correct start state. To do this, click ⊞ Set Start State in the Cognitive Controller Editor, and click the state that all delegates will start with. The default start state is the first state created.

If you want delegates to start with different states, you must set up the various cognitive controllers for each start state, and assign the appropriate delegates to each cognitive controller.

EXERCISE 12.2

Doing Simple Circular Transitions

In this exercise, you'll add a circular transition to the simple scene created in the last exercise.

1. Load the file SimpleCog02.max that you created earlier, or from the CD.

2. Select the Crowd helper and go to the Modify panel.

3. Click ⊞ Cognitive Controllers.

   The Cognitive Controller Editor appears, showing the graph you set up earlier.

4. Click ⊞ Create Transition, and click and drag from Circulate Right to Circulate Left to create a transition in the direction opposite the existing transition. This creates a circular transition between the states.

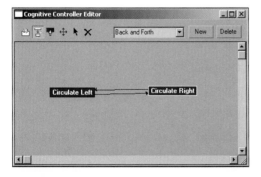

For the new transition, you will now create a transition script very similar to the first one. To make this easier, we'll copy and paste the first transition script.

5. Click ⬚ Select State/Transition.

6. Right-click the transition you set up earlier, the one from Circulate Left to Circulate Right, to open the transition editor.

7. On the transition editor, click Edit MAXScript.

8. In the MAXScript window, select the entire script and press Ctrl+C.

9. Close the MAXScript window, and close the transition editor.

10. Right-click the new transition from Circulate Right to Circulate Left.

11. Change Duration to 5.

12. Under Transition Condition, enter the name Trans2.

13. Click Edit MAXScript.

14. In the MAXScript window, press Ctrl+V to paste the script.

15. In the first line of the script, change Trans1 to Trans2.

16. Close the MAXScript window, and close the transition editor.

17. Close the Cognitive Controller Editor.

    The cognitive controller has already been assigned to the delegate, so there's no need to assign it again.

18. On the Solve rollout, click Solve.

    The delegate goes back and forth from one sphere to the other, every 50 frames. A finished example of this scene can be found in the file SIMPLECOG03.MAX on the CD.

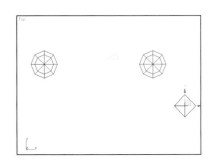

The MAXScript Listener

In the MAXScript Listener window, you can see reports of events in your script. The Listener will tell you what delegates are doing and whether they've gone through a transition. In general, it helps you keep track what's happening so you can make corrections if necessary.

To open the MAXScript Listener window, choose MAXScript Listener from the MAXScript menu, or press F11 on the keyboard.

You can include instructions in your script to print information to the Listener window. For example, the following line, when included in a script, prints the delegate's unique index:

```
print (del.index)
```

To print a specific line of text, include the text in quotation marks, like this:

```
print ("Your text here")
```

If you're interested in seeing all the delegate properties that can be used in a script, type this line into the MAXScript Listener window and press Enter:

```
ShowProperties $delegate01
```

EXERCISE 12.3

Making Delegates Stay or Fly

In this exercise, you'll set up a cognitive controller to make delegates fly away when a biped gets within a certain distance. For this animation, you'll need two states: one for when the delegates

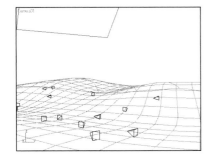

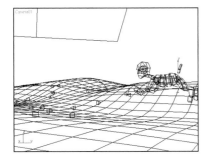

stay still, and another for when they fly away. We'll also experiment with some new behaviors to make the simulation

1. Load the file `Hill01.max` from the CD. If you get a Missing External Files error click Browse, find the DogwalkLoop.bip and Dogwalk.bip files, and then click Add, to resolve the problem.

   This file contains a hillside with several delegates scattered on it.

2. Unhide the named selection set Biped. This is the dog biped used in Chapter 7, "Animating with Freeform."

3. Play the animation.

   The dog biped walks into the scene and jumps in the direction of the delegates. A sphere named Sphere01 has been linked to the biped's head. When the distance between the sphere and a delegate falls below a certain number, the delegate will fly away.

4. Select the Crowd helper and go to the Modify panel.

5. On the Setup rollout, click New. Choose Speed Vary Behavior.

6. On the Speed Vary Behavior rollout, change Center to 0.

   This will cause delegates to stay put when following this behavior.

7. On the Setup rollout, click New. Choose Wall Seek Behavior.

8. On the Wall Seek Behavior rollout, under Grid to Seek, click the button, and click the grid (`Grid01`).

   When following this behavior, the delegates will seek the grid hovering above the terrain.

9. Uncheck the Use Distance checkbox. When Use Distance is on, the behavior activates only when the delegates are within the specified distance.

10. Click New, and choose Avoid Behavior.

11. On the Avoid Behavior rollout, click ⬛ Multiple Selection and choose all the delegates.

   This will keep the delegates from coming too close to one another. Notice that this does not yet assign the behavior, only the objects to be avoided.

Set Up Cognitive Controllers

Now you're ready to set up cognitive controllers that will determine when delegates follow each behavior. One of the states will include multiple behaviors.

1. On the Setup rollout, click ⬛ Cognitive Controllers.

2. Click New to start a new cognitive controller. Name the controller Flyaway.

3. Click twice in the Cognitive Controller Editor to create two states.

4. Click ⬛ Select State/Transition.

5. Right-click the State box.

6. In the State dialog, replace the name State with the name Stay.

7. Click Add, and choose Speed Vary.

   The Speed Vary behavior now defines the Stay state.

8. Click OK to close the Stay dialog.

9. Right-click the State1 box.

10. On the State1 dialog, change the name State1 to Fly.

11. Click Add, and choose the Avoid and Wall Seek behaviors.

   The Fly state is now defined as both the Avoid behavior and the Wall Seek behavior.

12. Click OK to close the Fly dialog.

Create the Transition

Now that both states are defined, we can set up the conditions under which they'll be used. This time, our transition script will include a line that sends information to the MAXScript Listener. That will make any necessary troubleshooting much easier.

1. In the Cognitive Controller Editor, click 🖳 Create Transition.

2. Click and drag from Stay to Fly to create a transition.

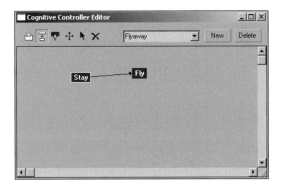

3. Click 🡅 Select State/Transition.

4. Right-click the transition line.

5. In the transition editor, change Duration to 3.

6. Change the Transition Condition name to Trans1.

7. Click Edit MAXScript.

8. On the MAXScript window, enter the following script:

```
fn Trans1 del t = (
get_dist = distance del.simpos $Sphere01.pos
print (get_dist)
if get_dist < 600 then 1 else 0
)
```

The distance function gets the distance between two objects in units, and puts it in the get_dist variable. The two objects being compared are the current delegate being tested, del, and the object Sphere01.

Then `get_dist` is tested; if it's less than 600 (meaning the delegate and Sphere01 are less than 600 units apart), the delegate will transition to the next state. Notice that `Sphere01` has a $ in front of it to indicate a direct reference to an object. The delegate reference, `del`, has no $ because it refers to whichever delegate is currently being compared, not to any specific delegate.

The third line, `print (get_dist)`, displays the current distance in the MAXScript Listener window.

9. Close the MAXScript window.

10. Click OK to close the transition editor.

11. Close the Cognitive Controller Editor.

Assign and Solve

The cognitive controller is all set up. Now you can assign it to delegates, and then solve and see how it looks.

1. On the Setup rollout, click ⬀ Behavior Assignments.

2. In the Behavior Assignments and Teams dialog, open the Teams section if necessary. Click New Team, and choose all the delegates.

3. In the Assignment Design section, highlight Team0 in the Teams list and Flyaway in the Cognitive Controllers list. Click the vertical bar of arrows to assign the cognitive controller to the team.

4. Click OK to close the dialog.

5. On the Solve rollout, change End Solve to `200`.

6. From the MAXScript menu choose MAXScript Listener to open the MAXScript Listener.

7. Click Solve in the Solve rollout.

Wait a few moments while the simulation is solved. The distances appear in the MAXScript Listener window to help you see how close the dog is getting to the delegates.

As the dog approaches, many of the delegates go from the Stay state to the Fly state.

8. Adjust the simulation as needed, and re-solve.

As mentioned before, it's very rare for a simulation to look just right on the first try. For example, your delegates might be arranged in such a way that the distance comparison of 600 is too much or too little. Try editing the Trans1 script and increasing the distance to 800 or 1000. Experiment with different values in the script to see which works best for your simulation.

9. Save the scene as Hill02.max.

Animation States

There may be times when you want a linked object to behave in a certain way, depending on what the delegate is doing. Consider a flying bird, for example. When the delegate is pitched a certain way or travels at a certain speed, you'd want the bird's wings to stay still so that the bird can glide. At other speeds or pitches, you'll want the bird to beat its wings. This type of control over the animation is accomplished with *animation states*.

First you set up a reference object, identical to those linked to delegates, with various frame ranges performing different motions.

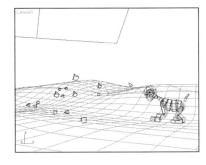

These frame ranges are called *clips*, and are used by animation states in much the same way that behavior states use behaviors. Each state is defined by various delegate attributes such as speed, acceleration, and pitch. When the delegate meets the designated criteria, the referenced clip is used on the linked object.

To set up animation states, you first animate the reference object. Take note of which frame ranges contain which animation. For example, frames 0–100 might contain one type of motion, while frames 110–180 might contain another.

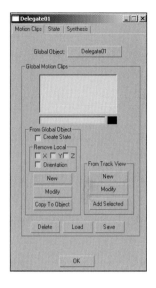

Next, you animate delegates in a crowd simulation. Make copies of the reference object, and align and link them to delegates with ⟲ Object/Delegate Associations.

Select the Crowd helper and go to the Modify panel. On the Global Clip Controllers rollout, click New, and choose the reference object. Highlight the reference object name in the Global Clip Controllers rollout, and click Edit. This opens the animation states dialog. In the Motion Clips tab of this dialog, you specify which clips to use and when.

To set up a clip, click New in the From Global Object section, in the middle-left of the animation states dialog. The MotionClip Parameters dialog appears.

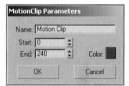

Enter a name for the clip, and its start and end frames; then click OK to close the dialog. Create a separate clip for each type of motion.

Back in the animation states dialog, use the other tabs to finish setting up the clip. On the State tab, set up individual states consisting of one or more clips. Click Edit Properties here to set up the conditions in which the state will be used, such as pitch, speed, and acceleration. The state will be used when the delegate's motion falls within the designated range.

On the Synthesis tab, click New Master Motion Clip to select all the linked objects that will be affected by animation states. Click Auto Blend All to automatically have the best blend points chosen for each pair of clips. Click Synthesize All to set animation states for each linked object based on delegate motion.

Tips for Using Animation States

When animating the reference object for use with animation states, keep these rules in mind.

- Function curves between all keys must be straight lines. Otherwise, you will not be able to select the objects when you click New Master Motion Clip (in the Synthesis tab of the animation states dialog).

- Animate with modifiers. Vertices animated at the Editable Mesh subobject level don't work with animation states. Get creative with Bend, Taper, Skew, Wave and other modifiers to make the needed motions.

- Make sure that there are several keys for each animated parameter all through the motion, not just at each end. The motion clip must have multiple keys, even if the reference object isn't moving or changing.

EXERCISE 12.4

Working with Bird Animation States

The use of animation states is best learned through practice. In this exercise, you'll link bird objects to the delegates in the hillside scene. When the birds are on the ground, they'll stand still or peck a little at the ground. When they fly away, they'll spread and beat their wings. You'll use animation states to make them behave correctly.

1. Load the scene `Hill02.max` that you created earlier, or from the CD.

2. Unhide the object Bird.

3. Zoom in on the Bird object.

4. Play the animation to see the bird's three types of motion:

    - In frames 0–130, the bird beats its wings.

    - In frames 130–215, the bird pecks at the ground.

    - In frames 215–255, the bird stands still.

Link Delegates

Now you'll use these motions to set up clips for animation states. Notice that there are several keys for these states, even for the last state where the bird stands still. These multiple keys are necessary so that transitions between states can be made smoothly. First, though, let's extend the length of the solved animation.

1. Select the Crowd helper, then on the Modify panel Solve rollout, change End Solve to 280.

2. Click Solve.

3. In any viewport, create 15 copies of the Bird object, named Bird01 through Bird15.

4. Select the Crowd helper and go to the Modify panel.

5. Click Object/Delegate Associations.

6. Under Objects, click Add, and choose Bird01 through Bird15.

7. Under Delegates, click Add, and choose all 15 delegates.

8. Click Align Objects with Delegates.

9. Click Link Objects to Delegates.

10. Click OK to close the dialog.

    The birds are now aligned and linked with delegates. The birds are positioned slightly above the delegates.

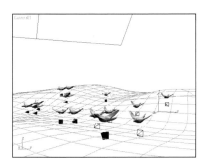

Set Up Animation States

Now we can set up clips for each of our three motions.

1. With the Crowd helper still selected, scroll down to the Global Clip Controllers rollout of the Modify panel.

> ►TIP◄
>
> When using animation states that test the speeds of delegates, you'll want to make sure the animation is solved to the end of the current animation length. Otherwise, delegates stop at the end of the simulation, and animation states interpret this as a speed of 0.

2. Click New, and choose the object Bird.

3. Highlight Bird in the Global Clip Controllers rollout, and click Edit.

   The animation states dialog for Bird appears.

4. At the middle-left of the dialog, in the From Global Object section, click New.

5. On the MotionClip Parameters dialog, enter the name Fly.

6. Enter 10 and 120 as the Start and End for the frame range.

   Even though the range goes from frame 0 to 130, animation states sometimes work better when you don't use the extreme ends of the motion range.

7. Click OK to close the MotionClip Parameters dialog.

8. Click New again in the animation states dialog. Enter Peck for the name, with a Start of 155 and End of 215. Click OK.

9. Click New again. Enter Stand for the name, with a Start of 225 and End of 255. Click OK.

10. Click the State tab of the animation states dialog for Bird.

11. Click New State, and enter the name Fly.

12. Click Add Clip, and choose the Fly clip.

13. Click New State again, and enter the name Stay.

14. Click Add Clip, and choose Peck and Stand.

    Even though these state names are the same as the states in the Cognitive Controller Editor, they are not related in any way. We're just using the same names here because they best describe the bird's activities.

15. In the Motion Clips list highlight the Peck clip, and change the MotionClip Weight to 80.

    This will make the birds more likely to stand than to peck.

Set Clip Criteria

Now that the clips are all set up, we can designate the properties that will control them and specify their ranges.

1. With the Stay state still selected, click Edit Properties.

    This opens the properties editor for the Stay state. Notice it has many different tabs for the various properties.

2. In the Speed tab, check the Use Speed checkbox.

3. For the Max value, enter 1.

    We want this state to be active when the delegate isn't moving. So we've set it to use the Speed property, and to be active only when the speed is between 0 and 1 units per frame.

4. Click Exit to leave the Stay dialog.

5. Click the State tab, then in the Synthesis States section choose the Fly state, and click Edit Properties.

    This state will be active when the delegate is moving. We'll set it to be active when the delegate is moving at a speed faster than 1 unit per frame.

6. In the properties editor Speed tab, check the Use Speed checkbox.

7. For the Min value, enter 1.

8. Click Exit to leave the Fly dialog.

Create the Simulation

The animation states are all set up, and we're ready to synthesize the motion.

1. Click the Synthesis tab of the animation states dialog for Bird.

2. Click New Master Motion Clip, and choose the objects Bird01 through Bird15. This assigns the synthesized motion to the cloned birds.

3. At the bottom-right of the tab, click Auto Blend All. This allows for smooth transitions between the motion clips.

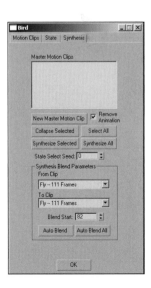

4. In the middle of the tab, click Synthesize All and wait a few moments while the motion is synthesized.

   In the first few frames, the birds settle into the standing state. Some of them peck a little. When the dog approaches, they spread their wings and fly.

5. Hide the delegates and play the animation.

6. Save your work as `Hill03.max`.

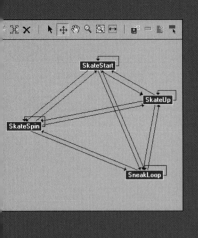

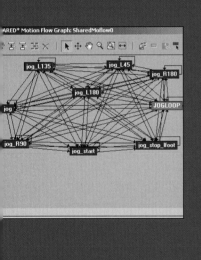

CHAPTER 13

Biped Crowds

Bipeds can be made to follow delegate behavior. In order for this to work, the bipeds must be created in the scene with the delegates, and must have a motion flow network for random motion and shared motion flow.

The secret to success with bipeds and crowds is all in the motion flow network. When a delegate needs to move forward, stop, or turn, Character Studio will look for a suitable clip (BIP file) to transition to. As a rule of thumb, at least eight clips are needed to make a good biped crowd scene that will solve well.

In this chapter, you'll learn to create scripts that randomize motion flow animation (see Chapter 10, "Motion Mixer and Motion Flow," if you need a refresher). Then you'll learn how biped crowd simulations are different from other biped animations. You'll then combine all your lessons from the last three chapters to create a crowd of jogging bipeds.

Working with Random Scripts

Random scripts are useful for groups of bipeds moving in a similar but not identical fashion. One Motion Flow Graph with multiple transitions can generate a different random script for each biped. An example of this arrangement would be bipeds in a cheering audience, or bipeds walking around a public area such as a train station.

Creating Multiple Transitions

When generating random scripts, Character Studio's Motion Flow requires more than one transition between clips so that it will have a variety to choose from. One option is to use the ⊞ Create All Transitions button in the Motion Flow Graph to automatically create a transition between each clip in both directions, as well as to create a transition from each clip to itself.

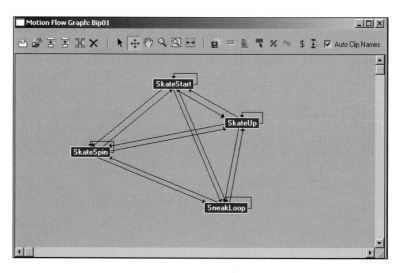

The transitions created automatically with Create All Transitions are the same as those created manually with either of the Create Transition buttons.

►QUICKLIST◄

RANDOM SCRIPTS ON MULTIPLE BIPEDS

❏ Select one biped, and click ⬚ Motion Flow Mode.

❏ Click ⬚ Show Graph to display the Motion Flow Graph.

❏ Load all clips to be used.

❏ Click ⊞ Create All Transitions in the Motion Flow Graph.

❏ Delete unwanted transitions.

❏ Select all transitions. Click ⬚ Optimize Selected Transitions.

❏ Manually edit transitions as necessary.

❏ Click Select Random Start Clips, and choose one or more clips.

❏ Click ⬚ Define Script, and choose a clip.

❏ Click ⬚ Save File to save the MFE file.

❏ Click ⬚ Shared Motion Flow. Choose the MFE file, and select bipeds.

❏ Click ⬚ Create Random Motion.

When should you use each method?

- In general, if you want to put transitions between most of the clips, use ⌘ Create All Transitions and then delete any unwanted transitions. To delete the unwanted transitions, select them with ▶ Select Clip/Transition, and click ✕ Delete Clip/Transition.

- If you want to create transitions between just a few clips, use ⊟ Create Transition To.

Synthesized transitions (transitions that are automatically created by the crowd software) can be optimized and edited in the same way as transitions created manually. It is recommended that you optimize synthesized transitions for the best results.

►NOTE◄

For full instructions on creating and optimizing transitions, see Chapter 10.

Note that creating a random script will randomize the *selection* of transitions. It will not randomize the *durations* of the transitions themselves, nor the starting and ending frames over which the transition occurs.

Before generating a random script, you'll need to select one or more clips as possible start clips for the motion. Click Select Random Start Clips and click a clip. To select more than one possible start clip, hold down the Ctrl key as you click the clips. Selected clip names turn purple, and a number appears next to each selected clip's name.

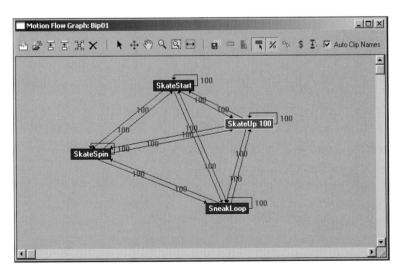

The number next to the clip name indicates the probability that the clip will be selected as the start clip. To change the probability, right-click the clip and in the transition editor change the Probability to a number from 0 to 100.

Notice that numbers also appear on the transition lines. These are *transition probabilities,* which you'll learn about later in this chapter.

There is another step required before random scripts can be generated. You must have a clip placed in the script in order to get started. This clip might be used as the starting clip when random scripts are generated, or it might not. It's only necessary that a clip, any clip, be placed in the script to get the process rolling.

When everything is in place and you're ready to generate the random script, click Define Script in the Scripts section of the Motion Flow rollout, and select a clip in the graph. The name of the clip appears in the Scripts section of the Motion Flow rollout. You're now ready to click Create Random Motion—as long as the script is for only one biped.

Shared Motion Flow for Multiple Bipeds

To generate random motion for multiple bipeds, you must first save an MFE file and then set up a *shared motion flow.* MFE files contain clips, transitions, and the script defined in the Scripts section of the Motion Flow rollout. (You don't need a saved MFE file in order to generate random motion for one biped only.) To save an MFE file, click ⬛ Save File in the Motion Flow rollout. By default, MFE files are saved in your \3dsMax8\Animations folder.

To set up shared motion flow, click ⊠ Shared Motion Flow in the Motion Flow rollout. In the Shared Motion Flow dialog, click the New button to create a new shared motion file. Then click Load.mfe, and choose the MFE file you created earlier.

Click Add, and select the bipeds to include in the shared motion flow. If the bipeds are different sizes, you'll receive a message telling you that the legs or other biped parts have the wrong scale. If this happens, simply click Reset Wrong Scales: Just Legs, or Reset Wrong Scales: Entire Figure to correct the problem.

If all the bipeds that share the motion flow aren't in motion flow mode in the Shared Motion Flow dialog, click ⊞ Put Multiple Bipeds in Motion Flow. This will put the bipeds in Motion Flow mode, which is recommended when working with motion flow.

Click OK to exit the Shared Motion Flow dialog. It will appear that nothing has happened, except that now the ⊞ Shared Motion Flow button in the Motion Flow rollout bears a white circle, indicating that the currently selected biped is included in a shared motion flow. A biped can be part of only one shared motion flow at any given time.

Generating Random Scripts

To generate scripts for one or more bipeds, click ⊞ Create Random Motion in the Scripts section of the Motion Flow rollout. The Create Random Motion dialog appears. This is where you'll set the basic parameters for the motion to be generated. Most are self-explanatory, but there are a few things to be aware of.

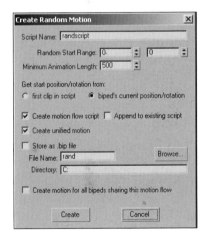

The Random Start Range can be used to vary the frames at which the bipeds will start moving. If you have fewer bipeds than you have clips, it's essential that you change these values to keep the motion random.

Notice that "Get start position/rotation from:" is set to "biped's current position/rotation." This will leave the bipeds in their original positions.

When the Create Unified Motion option is checked, the generated motion will be available for each biped even if you take it out of Motion Flow mode. This gives you the ability to manually change the biped's animation after the random script is generated, if necessary.

Click Create to start the creation process. Wait a few moments while the scripts are generated. The more bipeds you have in the shared motion flow, the longer this will take. Once the scripts have been generated, you can play the animation to see the motion.

EXERCISE 13.1

Making a Cheering Audience

In this exercise, you'll use two clips, SIT.BIP and CHEER.BIP, to create a scene with three bipeds cheering as if at a sporting event. To make their motion look more natural, you'll create a random script for their actions.

1. Copy the files SIT.BIP and CHEER.BIP from the CD to the \3dsmax8\Cstudio\Moflow folder on your hard disk. If this folder doesn't already exist on your hard drive, go ahead and create it. You'll need to have this file on your hard disk so that Character Studio can find it when generating random scripts.

2. Reset 3ds Max.

3. Create a biped of any size.

4. Select any part of the biped and go to the Motion panel.

5. In the General rollout, click 🖼 Load File. Then navigate to the \3dsmax8\Cstudio\Moflow folder and load the file SIT.BIP.

6. If the biped isn't visible in your viewports, click ⊞ Zoom Extents All to find it.

7. Play the animation.

   Not much happening here—the biped just sits.

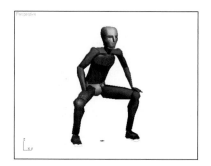

8. In the Biped rollout, click  Load File, and load CHEER.BIP.

9. Play the animation. The biped gets up and cheers.

10. Load the file Bleachers.max from the CD. This file contains a biped sitting in bleachers, as if at a sporting event.

    We'll want to make copies of this biped. But first, let's set keys for the COM.

11. Select the biped and go to the Motion panel.

    Click ⟷ Body Horizontal, and click ● Set Key.

    Click ↕ Body Vertical, and click ● Set Key.

    Click ↻ Body Rotation, and click ● Set Key.

    Now let's make two friends for the biped. In a complex scene, you'd want more than three bipeds, but we'll keep it simple for now.

12. Click ⟷ Body Horizontal, and click ✛ Select and Move.

13. Turn on the Auto Key button. (Having the Auto Key button on when cloning a biped sets the new position of the biped.)

14. In the Front viewport, make another biped by holding down the Shift key and moving the biped to its right.

15. Repeat the operation to create a third biped.

16. Turn off Auto Key.

    Let's change the sizes of the two new bipeds.

17. Select the second biped and click 🧍 Figure Mode.

18. In the Structure rollout, change the Height parameter to 930.

19. Click 🧍 Figure Mode again to turn it off.

20. Turn on Figure mode, change the Height of the third biped to 800, then turn off Figure mode.

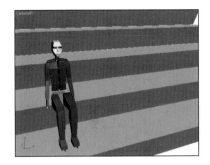

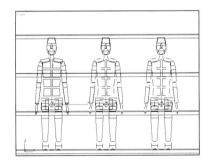

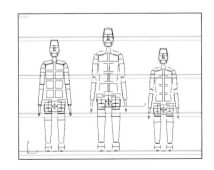

21. Before continuing, save the file as BLEACHERS01.MAX in your folder.

This last step is very important. You'll need the saved file later in order to make the animation work correctly.

Set Up the Script

Now you're ready to set up a script. Then you can pick a random start clip, start the script, and save the MFE file.

1. Select the first biped.

2. In the Motion panel, click ⬚ Motion Flow Mode.

3. In the Motion Flow rollout, click ⬚ Show Graph.

4. In the Motion Flow Graph, click ⬚ Create Multiple Clips. Navigate to the \3dsMax8\Cstudio\Moflow folder and choose the two clips CHEER.BIP and SIT.BIP and then click Open.

The two clips appear in the Motion Flow Graph.

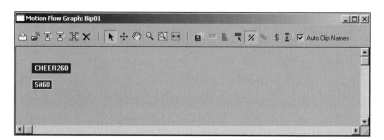

5. Use ⬚ Move Clip to move the clips apart.

6. With *both* clips selected, click ⬚ Create All Transitions. A dialog opens asking if transitions to the selected objects should also be created. Click Yes and continue.

Transitions appear between the clips, and from each clip to itself. Next, we'll optimize the transitions.

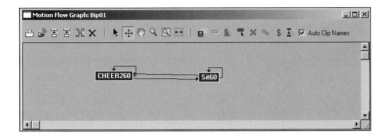

7. Click ▶ Select Clip/Transition, and drag a selection area around the clips and transitions, to select all transitions.

8. Click ✸ Optimize Selected Transitions. In the Transition Optimization dialog, choose Search Entire Clip, and click OK.

9. Click Select Random Start Clips, and click the SIT clip.

10. On the Scripts section of the Motion Flow rollout, click ⊠ Define Script, and click the SIT clip.

11. In the Motion Flow rollout, click ⊞ Save File. Save the MFE file with the name SPORTS.MFE in the \3dsMax8\Cstudio\Moflow folder.

Set Up Shared Motion Flow

You're just about ready to set up shared motion flow. But first, let's take a look at a small problem that has arisen. The selected biped has moved to the position of the SIT clip that was placed in the Motion Flow script. If you generate random scripts now, the biped will start from this position. To solve this problem, we can go back to the saved version of the file and apply the shared motion flow to that file. There is no need to save the current file— the only thing that has changed is the creation of the graph and script, which we just saved as SPORTS.MFE.

1. Reload the file BLEACHERS01.MAX that you saved earlier.

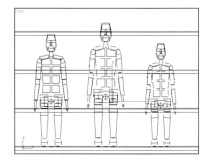

2. Select any biped and click ⛷ Motion Flow Mode.

3. In the Motion Flow rollout, click ⊞ Shared Motion Flow.

4. In the Shared Motion Flow dialog, click New.

5. Click Load.mfe, and choose the file SPORTS.MFE.

6. Click Add, and choose all three bipeds.

   You'll see a message telling you that some of the leg scales are wrong. Click OK to continue.

7. In the Shared Motion Flow dialog, click Reset Wrong Scales: Just Legs.

8. Click OK to exit the dialog.

Create Random Motion

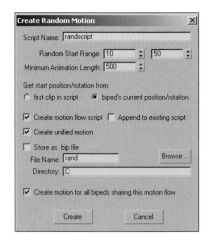

Time to create the random motion! It's a good idea to save the file in its current state first, in case you need to regenerate the motion.

1. Save the scene with the filename BLEACHERS02.MAX.

2. Click ▨ Create Random Motion in the Scripts section of the Motion Flow rollout.

3. In the Create Random Motion dialog, change the Random Start Range to be 10–50.

4. At the bottom of the dialog, check "Create motion for all bipeds sharing this motion flow."

5. Click the Create button to begin the creation process. In the Unify Options dialogs that appear, click OK.

6. When the message appears telling you that some bipeds are not in Motion Flow mode, click Yes to put them all in Motion Flow mode.

7. When the scripts have been created, play the animation.

   The bipeds randomly sit or get up and cheer.

8. Save the scene with the filename BLEACHERS03.MAX.

Tips for Random Scripts on Multiple Bipeds

Before generating random scripts, position the bipeds in their initial locations, and set a key on frame 0 for Body Horizontal, Body Vertical, and Body Rotation. Otherwise, these settings will come from the first BIP file in the script, which will probably place the biped somewhere else.

Once the bipeds are positioned, save the MAX file before going into Motion Flow mode. You'll need this, because the biped you use to set up the Motion Flow Graph will get moved in the process. You'll want to be able to get back to your original setup before generating random scripts.

Transitions work best when logical transition points exist between clips. This requires that you create your BIP files with care. One way to ensure accuracy is to create all the BIP files for a shared motion flow from a base BIP file.

Even with just two clips, you can add interest to the animation by placing the clip in the Motion Flow Graph more than once, and creating transitions of different lengths.

Transition Probabilities

When a transition is created, it is assigned a default *probability percentage* of 100. This probability assignment determines how likely the transition is to be chosen during random script generation.

To see probability values on the Motion Flow Graph, click ▣ Show Random Percentages. The probability appears on each transition line.

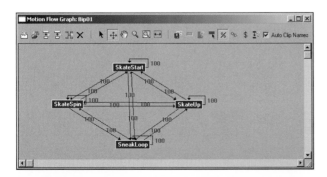

To change a transition's probability, select the transition and right-click it to display the transition editor. Change the Probability parameter at the upper right corner of the dialog, and click OK to close it. The new Probability value appears on the transition line.

When all transitions have the same probability, as with the default probability of 100, they all have the same chance of being chosen. When setting up multiple transitions for random scripts, you'll most likely want to change some of the probabilities, to decrease a particular transition's chance of being used.

In practice, you can take an educated guess as to the best transition probabilities before generating the first set of random scripts. It's not unusual to find that you need to return to the Motion Flow Graph and make adjustments to transition probabilities after seeing what has been generated.

EXERCISE 13.2

Making the Bipeds Sit More

At present, the bipeds in our cheering scene do a lot of cheering and very little sitting. To increase the chances that they'll sit rather than cheer, you can reduce the probability of transitions to the cheering motion.

1. Load the file BLEACHERS03.MAX that you made earlier.

2. Select any biped, go to the Motion panel, and click ⚂ Motion Flow Mode.

3. Click ⚃ Show Graph.

4. Click ⚃ Select Clip/Transition.

5. Right-click the transition from SIT to CHEER.

6. In the transition editor, change the Probability value to 10. Then click OK.

7. Right-click the transition from CHEER to itself.

8. Change the Probability value to 10, and click OK to close the dialog.

9. Click 📄 Save File and save the file as SPORTS2.MFE.

10. Save the Max file with the name BLEACHERS04.MAX.

11. Click 📄 Shared Motion Flow.

12. Click Load.mfe and choose SPORTS2.MFE.

13. Click OK to close the dialog.

14. Click Create Random Motion.

15. In the Create Random Motion dialog, change the Random Start Range to go from 10 to 50, if it isn't already set to those values.

16. Check "Create motion for all bipeds sharing this motion flow." And then click Create. Click OK in the Unify Options dialog each time it appears.

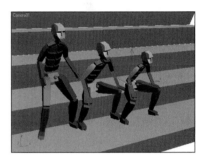

17. Wait a few moments while the random scripts are created.

18. Play the animation.

    The bipeds are now much more likely to sit than cheer. When they do cheer, they sit right back down again.

Edit Transitions

Right now, the bipeds always transition between sitting and cheering in the same way. We'll add another set of clips to create some variety.

1. Locate CHEER260.BIP and SIT60.BIP from the MOTIONS folder on the CD and copy them to the \CStudio\Moflow directory as before. Then load the file BLEACHERS04.MAX that you created earlier.

2. Select any biped and go to the Motion panel.

3. Click 🔲 Motion Flow Mode, if it isn't already turned on.

4. On the Motion Flow rollout, click 🔲 Show Graph.

5. Click ⬚ Create Multiple Clips, and choose the files SIT60.BIP and CHEER260.BIP.

   Two new clips are created.

6. Create transitions between SIT60 and CHEER260 using the Create Transition From > To buttons. Also create transitions from SIT to CHEER260 and from SIT60 to CHEER. Be sure to also create transitions for the new clips back to themselves (SIT60 to SIT60 and CHEER260 to CHEER 260).

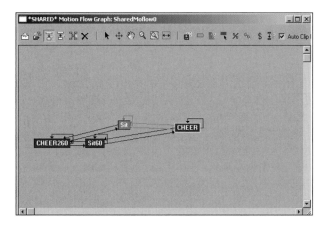

7. Right-click the transition going from SIT to CHEER260.

   You can see whether you chose the right transition because SIT —> CHEER260 appears at the top of the transition editor.

   This transition starts at frame 36 of the SIT clip and frame 0 of the CHEER260 clip, and has a Length of 10 frames.

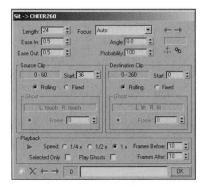

8. Click OK to close the transition editor.

9. Right-click the transition line from CHEER260 to SIT60.

   This transition starts at frame 233 of the CHEER260 clip and frame 0 of the SIT60 clip, and lasts 10 frames.

10. Click Select Clip/Transition.

11. Right-click the transition from CHEER2601 to SIT60.

12. Change the Start frame for the Source Clip to 100, and click OK.

Now the new Motion Graph is ready to be used with Motion Flow.

13. Click ⬜ Save File, and save the file as SPORTS3.MFE.

14. Click ⬜ Shared Motion Flow.

15. Click Load.mfe and choose SPORTS3.MFE.

16. Click OK to close the dialog.

17. Save the file as BLEACHERS05.MAX.

18. Click ⬜ Create Random Motion.

19. Change the Random Start Range to go from 10 to 50.

20. Check "Create motion for all bipeds sharing this motion flow" and then click Create. Click OK on the Unify Options dialog, as many times as it appears.

   Wait a few moments while the random scripts are created.

21. Play the animation.

   The bipeds now cheer for randomly long or short periods, sitting in between cheers.

22. Save the scene with the filename BLEACHERS06.MAX.

Adjusting Position

When you generate the random motion, you may notice that some of the bipeds have sunk into the bleachers. Since 3ds Max isn't using physics here, there is nothing to prevent the random motion from relocating the bipeds into a position where they intersect with the bleachers.

Fortunately, it's easy to fix this. In the Scripts section of the Motion Flow rollout, beneath the scripts list are fields for Start Position X, Y, and Z. You can enter 0 in the Start Position Z field to return the biped to a start position that doesn't intersect with the bleacher. Also, you can adjust the Start Position Y and X fields if the intersection is still visible after fixing the Z value. Select each biped and repeat this procedure to correct them all.

Editing Multiple Transitions

You can edit transitions either from Motion Flow Graph or from the script in the Scripts section of the Motion Flow rollout. Editing from the script gives you the ability to see the ghost skeleton for each clip, which is very helpful in making the best transition. However, with multiple transitions, the script won't be generated until later on.

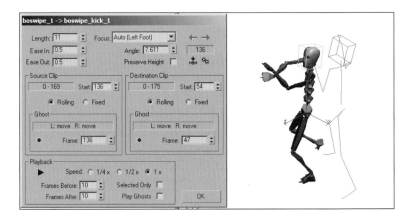

If you want to use the ghost skeleton to edit a transition on a multiple-transition graph, just set up a temporary script with the two clips. Click ⬚ Define Script on the Scripts section of the Motion Flow rollout, choose Create new script and then click the two clips in the Motion Graph. Highlight the first clip on the Scripts section of the Motion Flow rollout, and click ⬚ Edit Transition. You can now edit the transition with the ghost skeleton. The biped will move to the position in world space indicated by the BIP file, so you might have to search around to find it.

A change made to a transition on the Scripts section of the Motion Flow rollout instantly affects the transition on the Motion Flow Graph. You can repeat this process for as many clips as you'd like, to edit the transitions between them.

►NOTE◄

See Chapter 10 for more detailed information on defining scripts and creating transitions.

Using Motion Flow with Crowds

If you want to create a scene with bipeds walking or running about, you'll need to prevent them from bumping into one another. In this case, you should use Motion Flow in conjunction with Character Studio's Crowd tools. With the Crowd features, you can animate large groups of bipeds moving about, while at the same time preventing them from colliding and regulating where they go.

Once the bipeds and delegates are set up, the rest is easy. To associate bipeds with delegates, select the Crowd helper and go to the Modify panel. Click Biped/Delegate Associations. In the Associate Bipeds with Delegates dialog, under Bipeds, click Add and then choose the bipeds to associate with delegates. Under Delegates, click Add and choose the delegates. Click Associate to complete the process, and the bipeds will be associated with the delegates.

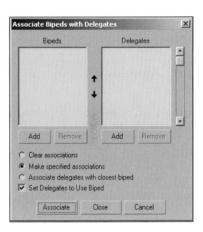

The bipeds won't move to the delegates immediately. Once you have set up the association between the Delegates and the Bipeds, go to the Solve rollout. Click Solve, and the simulation will calculate. When you solve the simulation, the bipeds will move to the delegates' starting positions. As the simulation is solved, the motion flow network will be used to choose various clips as the simulation rolls along.

Making an Effective Flow Graph

In order to make an effective Motion Flow Graph, you need to have an ample library of clip motions included on the graph. Any potential motion that the biped might need in your animation should be represented as a clip. Turns to the left or right, sudden stops, arm movements—all need to be represented by a `.bip` file in the Motion Flow Graph. As a rule, make sure you have at least eight files included, with transitions between all. It's a good idea to visit each transition and review it, to make sure the program did a good job of picking the right transition length.

While you're in the Motion Flow Graph, turn on ▣ Show Random Percentages; this lets you see the transition probability displayed as a number. Move the graph elements apart if you have problems inspecting the values. The transitions are assigned 100 as a default value, but you may want to assign a lower percentage to motions that cause the biped to stop.

It's not a bad idea to actually load all the BIP files one at a time, and play them to inspect their motion. For example, you can load all the BIP files used for the jogger simulation in Exercise 13.3. You'll see jogging looped, jogging turning 45 degrees to the right, jogging turning 90 degrees to the right, and similar files for left turns.

Biped Priorities

For complex crowd work, you can prioritize the biped/delegate association solving. If a group of characters are running over a hill, prioritize the characters in front to solve before the characters that follow them. This makes sense and prevents some collisions between characters.

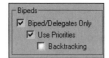

In the Solve rollout, in the Bipeds section, click Biped/Delegates Only.

This makes Use Priorities available as a choice. Click Use Priorities, and then you can use the tools in the Priority rollout to assign priorities to delegates in the viewport.

You can select a Start Priority, and then assign that priority to the delegate in the viewport. You do this by using the Pick/Assign button in the Assign by Picking section of the Priority rollout. Remember that the lower the number, the higher the priority. Zero trumps one; zero goes first.

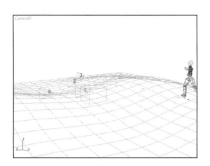

If Display Priorities is turned on at the bottom of the Priority rollout, you can see the delegate priorities as numbers in the viewport.

You can also assign priorities computationally, rather than by picking delegates. Priorities can be assigned based on a proximity to a grid of objects, to speed the work of assigning delegates when you have larger numbers in your crowd simulation.

The Use Priorities feature also allows for a Backtracking algorithm to be turned on. When Backtracking is clicked, the Solve computation will "rewind" back to the start frame and try out multiple solutions until it finds the best one. This will take more time for the computation, but it should result in an improved choice of motion for each biped/delegate association.

If you turn Backtracking on, you'll see that during the solve operation the simulation engine tries on multiple solutions. Watch the time slider, and you can see the simulation engine skipping back in time again and again in order to ascertain the preferred outcome. What is actually happening is that a motion script is being written for each biped, to correlate the delegate movement with the appropriate choice from the library of possible motions.

EXERCISE 13.3

Create Jogging Bipeds

1. Copy the file `JOGGING.MFE` from the `\motions` folder on the CD to the `3dsMax8\Cstudio\Moflow` folder on your hard disk. Also copy all the BIP files that start with "jog" as well. There are 12 of these, which comprise a library of possible jogging motions.

2. Load the file `JOGGERS.MAX` from the CD. If you get a Missing External Files error, navigate to the various jogging BIP files you just copied to resolve it.

   This scene contains a crowd simulation with four delegates moving over a bumpy surface. The delegates seek the box at the center of the surface while avoiding each other.

   The scene also contains four bipeds. They have each been set up with a dense Motion Flow network of jogging actions. Because all have the same network and the same starting clip, they're all on top of one another. If you want to see the network, select any part of a biped and go to the Motion panel. Click Motion Flow Mode, and click Show Graph.

3. Select the Crowd helper and go to the Modify panel.

4. Click Biped/Delegate Associations.

5. Under Bipeds, click Add and choose the four bipeds.

6. Under Delegates, click Add and select the four delegates.

7. Click Associate. Nothing changes in the viewport.

8. In the Solve rollout click Solve.

   While the solving is in progress, the bipeds jog over the terrain, following the delegates, turning to avoid one another while seeking the box. Save your file as myjoggingcrowd.max.

Prioritize the Joggers

You can't undo the crowd simulation solution, so instead we'll have you load a different MAX file.

1. Load Joggers_priorities.max from the CD.

2. Select the Crowd object. On the Modify panel, find the Bipeds group of the Solve rollout.

3. Turn on Biped/Delegates Only; then click Use Priorities.

4. In the Priority rollout, click the Pick/Assign button in the Assign by Picking section.

5. In the Top viewport, click on the delegate you'd like to solve first.

6. Click on the other delegates in the order you prefer.

   The delegate priority numbers should appear in the viewport as you click. If you don't see them, make sure Display Priorities is turned on at the bottom of the Priority rollout.

7. Click Solve.

   This time, the biped/delegate associations solve one at a time. You can see that each biped follows the motion of the delegate. At any given frame, it's possible for any of the motions in the Shared Motion Graph to be used. The simulation makes these choices during the solve operation, one biped at a time.

Use Backtracking

If you want to try out different setting choices and solve repeatedly, turn on Delete Keys Before Solve in the Solve rollout. This setting gives you a clean start each time.

1. In the Solve rollout, turn on Delete Keys Before Solve.

2. Now in the Bipeds group, turn on Backtracking.

3. Click Solve.

   You can see the simulation engine trying on numerous motion clips for each biped until a choice is made. This takes substantially longer than the earlier solves, because it is trying on many more possibilities. Leave the simulation alone and let it finish its work; eventually it will make up its mind.

4. Hide the delegate objects; then play the animation. If the bipeds run off the screen, move the camera as needed to get a better view.

   Examine the animation, and you can see that in the beginning the joggers appear to be jogging almost in unison. This can be changed easily.

5. Select any biped in the scene.

6. In the Motion panel, open the Motion Flow rollout and highlight 0000:JOGLOOOP at the top of the script list.

7. Change the Start Frame to a different number.

8. Repeat this alteration for each biped in the scene.

9. Play the animation.

   The bipeds are no longer doing synchronized running, and the animation appears more natural.

10. Save your file as MYJOGGERS.max.

RESOURCES

Files

3ds Max comes with a number of meshes, available on the DVD.

Numerous `BIP` files come with Character Studio. You'll find them on the 3ds Max DVD in the following folders:

- `\Samples\Motions\Bip\`

  This folder contains 19 subfolders that have categories of `BIP` files such as Dance, Fight, March, and so on.

- `\tutorials\character animation`

  The 3ds Max tutorials subdirectories contain many `BIP` files.

> **►NOTE◄**
>
> 3ds Max 8 ships on a single DVD. The Character Studio `BIP` files are on the DVD, but they do not install when you install 3ds Max. You'll have to manually copy them to your local hard drive.

Web Sites

These Web sites have free or inexpensive character models:

www.turbosquid.com

www.3dcafe.com

www.3dkingdom.org

And this site offers links to many others, for 3D models, software, and more:

www.digitaldreamdesigns.com/3DModels.htm

Books

These are just a few of the many books on 3D modeling that can help you out.

Model, Rig, Animate with 3ds max 7, Michele Bousquet (New Riders, 2005)

Modeling a Character in 3DS Max, Second Edition, Paul Steed (Wordware Publishing, 2005)

3ds max 6 Animation: CG Filmmaking from Concept to Completion, Barrett Fox (McGraw-Hill Osborne Media, 2003)

Game Character Modeling and Animation with 3ds max 7, Yancey Clinton (CMP Books, 2005)

Building a Digital Human, Ken Brilliant (Charles River Media, 2003)

Advanced 3ds max 5 Modeling & Animating, Boris Kulagin (A-List Publishing, 2003)

INDEX